Minnesota Heritage Cookbook

VOLUME I

hand-me-down recipes

"Heritage"
anything that is passed on to one's heirs or to generations that succeed . . .

"A Family Heirloom"
from generation to generation . . .

"Edible Nostalgia"
a strong desire for old fashioned taste treats . . .

"A Culinary Legacy"
from the kitchens of our ancestors . . .

for the benefit of

AMERICAN CANCER SOCIETY®
Minnesota Division, Inc.

The **Minnesota Heritage Cookbook** was an instant hit when it came out 100,000 copies ago, because the recipes were proven favorites gathered from a state of good cooks. Now a decade later it's still proving it's appeal as a bible of Minnesota tastes.

Eleanor Ostman
Foodwriter, St. Paul Pioneer Press

It is exciting to see one of my favorite cookbooks back in print. It was a classic when it was created and it remains a classic today. For a whole new generation of cooks and cookbook collectors, this cookbook is a must.

Helen Hays
Director of Marketing and Public Relations
Favorite Recipes® Press

The **Minnesota Heritage Cookbook Volume I** committee is proud and thrilled to receive the McIlhenny Cookbook Hall of Fame Award for community cookbooks that have sold over 100,000 copies. Now the second edition is off and running to win more awards and inspire more cooks while raising funds to support the fight against cancer.

Sue Zelickson, Editor
Minnesota Heritage Cookbook
WCCO Radio Food Reporter

Updated nutritional information on pages 156–160.
Recipes can be adjusted to meet specific American Cancer Society guidelines.

Published by the American Cancer Society, Minnesota Division, Inc.
3316 West 66th Street, Minneapolis, Minnesota 55435
612/925-2772   1/800/582-5152 (MN only)

Produced by Favorite Recipes® Press
P.O. Box 305142
Nashville, Tennessee 37230
1/800/358-0560

here we are

table of contents

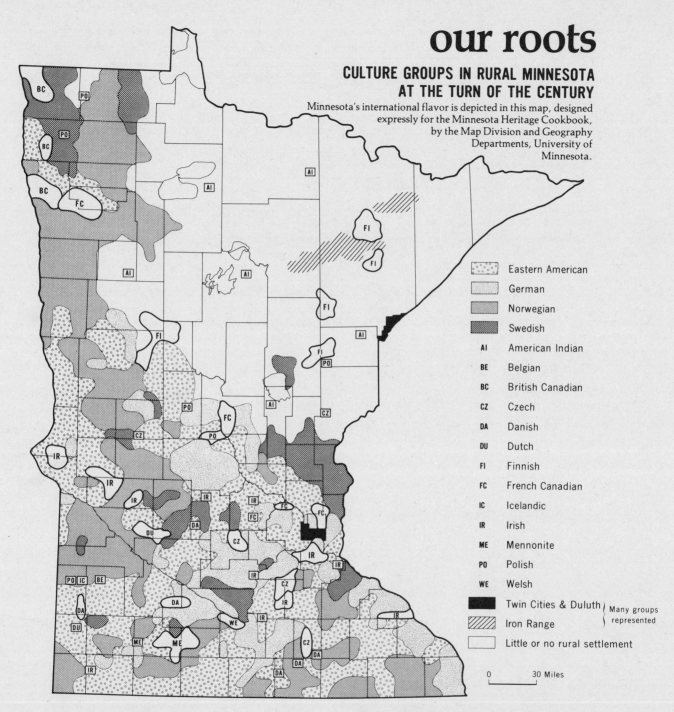

our roots

CULTURE GROUPS IN RURAL MINNESOTA AT THE TURN OF THE CENTURY

Minnesota's international flavor is depicted in this map, designed expressly for the Minnesota Heritage Cookbook, by the Map Division and Geography Departments, University of Minnesota.

Legend:

- Eastern American
- German
- Norwegian
- Swedish
- AI — American Indian
- BE — Belgian
- BC — British Canadian
- CZ — Czech
- DA — Danish
- DU — Dutch
- FI — Finnish
- FC — French Canadian
- IC — Icelandic
- IR — Irish
- ME — Mennonite
- PO — Polish
- WE — Welsh
- Twin Cities & Duluth } Many groups represented
- Iron Range
- Little or no rural settlement

0   30 Miles

4

heritage map

To say you're a Minnesotan is not quite enough. You can't say you really know Minnesota, if you don't know its people.

We delight in the stories about growing up on the Iron Range or tramping through the great North Woods. We reminisce about the camaraderie on the "Nordeast" side and we rejoice at the welcome sound of native tongues in Floodwood and New Ulm. We love to hear about the three-month journeys across the Atlantic from every corner of the Old World. We are in awe of the settlers who cleared the land for 25 cents a day and the optimistic merchants who started businesses on the Main Streets that dot every small town across the state.

We long for the nearness of the "old neighborhood" and nourishments of our ethnic roots, yet most of us have been transplanted. We are miles away and generations removed from grandma's kitchen, so we must turn to memories of her cookie jar and bread box to fill the void.

Those treasured recipes seem to awaken our senses, from the wondrous sights of smorrebrød to the sizzling sound of potato pancakes hitting the frying pan.

Whether it's the heavenly aroma of fresh-baked ginger cookies or the pungent odor of cooked cabbage, the old favorites just seem to lead us around by the nose.

As recipes started coming in from all corners of the state, we quickly realized that we are all brothers and sisters under the dough; the spaetzle, the won ton, the kreplach, the pierogi and the piroshki unite us all.

May many marvelous memories come alive with this collection of delectable edible nostalgia. We hope that you will enjoy these culinary legacies and turn them into your own hand-me-down recipes.

foreword

food for thought

Minnesota Heritage Cookbook

1 large volunteer project to benefit the American Cancer Society

50 active committee members

7000 recipe requests, mailed across the state

100's of recipe contributors, testers and helpers (see page 168)

186 brave hungry tasters

1 dozen busy staff from A.C.S. Minnesota Division

3 marvelous map designers

4 terrific typists, with 40 tender fingers

8 bright eyed editors and proofers

2 generous paper suppliers

4 creative artists

2 fantastic printers

78 strong shoulders to lean on

1 year of dedication and patience

dash of understanding spouses

pounds of input and sense of humor

1 large public relations network

1000 workers and outlets for distribution
sprinkle with sympathetic friends and families, adding more to season as time goes on . . .

Mix above ingredients carefully, in order given. Blend well, making sure not to over work. Simmer for 11-12 months, stirring constantly. Bake in 80 x 450 square foot printer's building over low heat. Check progress periodically. Remove and distribute widely throughout the country for the benefit of the American Cancer Society.

yield:

15,000 first batch

15,000 second batch

20,000 third batch

15,000 fourth batch

15,000 fifth batch

10,000 sixth batch

5,000 seventh batch

5,000 eighth batch

10,000 ninth batch

Total: 110,000 in print

Multitudes of thanks to all the "Very Special People" who gave time, talent, flavor and expertise to this quality product. It is done to perfection because you cared. For those of you who take a taste, we hope that you will enjoy reading and eating these delicious recipes and thank you all for the help and support you are giving the American Cancer Society.

Editor: Sue Zelickson

Assistant Editors: Betsy Norum, Francie Paper, Delores Sigel

Foreword: Bonnie Miller Rubin

Heritage Map: Sandra Haas, John Rice, Jon Walstrom

Coordinators

Ruth Abry, Judy Anderson, Bernice Berg, Vivian Berkstedt, Pat Breitenstein, Barbara Bunn, Ann Burckhardt, Bonnie Carlson, Leeann Chin, Rusty Cohen, Dottie Dekko, Joan Dizon, Jane Eschweiler, Debby Frenzel, Pam Graff, Kay Haaland, DeeDee Harris, Judy Hilger, Peggy Hitt, Marge Hogenson, Nan Holland, Sharon Howell, Liz Joseph, Helene Kaplan, Dalia Katz, Beverly Kees, Ann Knelman, Lois Lee, Sandra Linderholm, Donna Lien Miller, Yvonne Moody, Betty Myhre, Evelyn Nahurski, Susan Stuart-Otto, Helen Quinn, Claudia Reagen, Jo Robins, Harriette Rutstein, Lonnie Sachs, Roxanne Sands, Judie Weil.

Additional Contributors, Testers and Helpers (see page 168).

in the beginning

appetizers & soups

Scandinavian
Gravlaks

Dilled Fresh Salmon

1 salmon, cut horizontally and
    boned, but not skinned (thus in
    two large fillets)
1 tsp. white pepper
¼ c. sugar
¼ c. coarse Kosher salt
4 oz. cognac
2 oz. sherry
4 T. fresh dill (1 large bunch)

Lay one fillet of fish, skin side
down, in a dish just large enough
to contain it. In separate bowl,
combine the pepper, sugar and
salt. Rub this mixture evenly over
the fish. Splash on the cognac and
sherry. Spread dill over the salmon. Place second fillet over first,
flesh to flesh; cover with waxed
paper and place a heavy platter or
board on it. Weight the platter
with 3 or 4 heavy cans. Refrigerate 12-24 hours, basting 2 or 3
times with the liquid that accumu-
lates. (Fish can be allowed to
marinate as long as 4 to 6 days,
depending on your preference of
flavor.)

To serve, transfer to serving
platter (both fillets should be
arranged skin side down), scrape
away dill, seasonings and any
trace of marinade and pat dry
with paper towels. Slice paper-
thin, detaching each slice from the
skin. May be garnished with
capers, minced onion or chopped
hard-cooked egg. Serve with Mustard Sauce (see index) and thinly
sliced black bread.

Gravlaks will keep up to 2
weeks in refrigerator.

20-30 servings

The Scandinavian version of lox.

Icelandic
Herring Salad

1 lb. pickled herring
1 (16 oz.) jar beets, chopped
1 c. mayonnaise
1 c. whipped cream
1 medium onion, thinly sliced
3 apples, peeled and chopped
2 medium potatoes, boiled and
    chopped (optional)
4 hard-cooked eggs, cut into
    eighths

Drain herring on paper towel and
cut into small pieces. Combine all
ingredients, adding eggs last;
chill. Serve in a glass bowl with
thin buttered pumpernickel
bread.

20-24 servings

As a first course serve in lettuce cups.

Italian
Olive Hors d'oeuvre

1 lb. Moroccan olives with red pepper
1 lb. Sicilian green olives
1 lb. ripe Greek olives
8 oz. fresh mushrooms, diced
1 large onion, diced
4 stalks celery, diced
1 carrot, diced
2 (16 oz.) jars pickled mild or hot pepper slices, drained
1½ T. oregano
½ T. dried basil
3 oz. olive oil
1 tsp. salt
½ tsp. freshly ground pepper

Pit olives; cut into halves or thirds. Combine diced mushrooms, onion, celery, carrot and drained peppers. Add remaining ingredients. Let stand for 2 hours, mixing thoroughly every 20 minutes. Serve in a bowl; fork onto Italian bread or sesame crackers.

16-20 servings

Moroccan and Sicilian olives are available at Italian food markets.

Roumanian
Pot L'jel

Eggplant Relish

1 large eggplant
½ medium Bermuda onion, minced
1 green pepper, seeded and minced
½ cucumber, minced
½ tsp. freshly ground pepper
1 tsp. salt
1 T. plus 1 tsp. vegetable or olive oil
1 T. plus 1 tsp. lemon juice
1 clove garlic, mashed (optional)

Prick eggplant skin in several places *before* baking to prevent bursting. Place whole unpeeled eggplant on cookie sheet and bake in 400 degree oven about 35-45 minutes or until black and wrinkled on outside and tender inside. Let eggplant cool until it can be handled. Cut in half, scoop out insides into a bowl; discard skin. Drain off any excess moisture. Mash thoroughly with fork or potato masher. Add all other ingredients; mix well. Season to taste. Serve as appetizer or salad with crackers or cocktail rye bread.

Yield about 1 quart

You don't have to be Roumanian to love eggplant this way.

Vietnamese
Shrimp Toast

¼ lb. shrimp, chopped very fine
¼ lb. finely ground pork
½ onion, minced
½ c. flour
4 eggs
1 tsp. salt
1 tsp. sugar
dash white pepper
6-8 slices French bread, cut ¼"- ½" thick
oil for frying

Mix first eight ingredients together thoroughly and spread on bread slices. Heat oil 350-375 degrees and fry pieces, shrimp side up, coaxing with fork to keep upright, about 1 minute. Turn shrimp side down and fry until golden brown. Increase heat and cook about 6 minutes more. Drain on paper towel and serve hot. This can be done ahead and reheated in a 400 degree oven for 5-10 minutes.

6-8 servings

Italian
Caponata Bua

Eggplant Appetizer

1 large eggplant
3-4 oz. olive oil
1 onion, minced
3 cloves garlic, mashed
2 green peppers, seeded and
   chopped
1 c. chopped celery
1 (8 oz.) can pitted black olives,
   drained and quartered
1 c. chopped mushroom pieces
4 oz. tomato paste
1 T. red wine vinegar
3 T. brown sugar
salt
freshly ground pepper

Dice unpeeled eggplant into ½″ cubes and soak in salted water for 1 hour. Pour off water, drain well and dry with paper towels. In large heavy skillet, heat olive oil. Add onion and garlic and saute over moderate heat until onion is translucent. Add eggplant, green peppers and celery. Cook covered, stirring occasionally for about 15 minutes. Add olives, mushrooms and tomato paste, thoroughly mixing paste with pan liquid. Add vinegar, brown sugar and simmer uncovered until all ingredients are tender, about 15 minutes. Season with salt and pepper to taste. Transfer to serving bowl and refrigerate. Serve at room temperature with sesame crackers or Italian bread. May also be served warm as a vegetable dish.

4-8 servings

Italian
Neapolitan Mushrooms

30 large mushrooms, cleaned and
   dried
3 oz. olive oil
½ lb. sauteed Italian sausage,
   spicy or mild, casings removed
1 c. seasoned Italian bread
   crumbs
4 oz. tomato paste
2 cloves garlic, mashed
2 oz. grated Romano or Parmesan
   cheese
freshly ground pepper

Remove stems and rub mushroom tops with olive oil. Combine sauteed sausage, crumbs, tomato paste, garlic and cheese; mix thoroughly. Fill cavities of mushrooms with mixture and place in shallow baking dish which has been rubbed with olive oil. Sprinkle additional grated cheese, any remaining olive oil and pepper over mushrooms and bake in 375 degree oven for 15-20 minutes.

Yield 2½ dozen

Finger food — so don't forget the napkins.

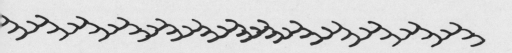

Chinese
Paper-Wrapped Fish

English
Hot Mushroom Turnovers

1 lb. fish fillet (walleye or any
    white, firm-fleshed fish)
1 T. vegetable oil
1 tsp. dark soy sauce
1 tsp. salt
¼ tsp. sesame oil
¼ tsp. white pepper
½ tsp. sugar
2 tsp. white wine
1 tsp. minced ginger root
2 green onions, cut in 2″ lengths,
    including green tops
20-30 5″ squares of parchment
    paper or aluminum foil
5 c. vegetable oil for frying

Cut fish into ½″ cubes; combine
next nine ingredients and pour
over fish cubes. Marinate for 1
hour. Place 2 pieces of fish with 1
piece of onion in center of parchment square. Fold into triangle.
Bring right and left corners of
triangle together to overlap over
filling. Bring top point down and
tuck behind overlapped sides.
Fish must be sealed securely inside
wrapper. Pour oil into wok or
heavy saucepan and heat to 375
degrees. Carefully place 10
wrapped fish packets into hot oil.
Fry about 3 minutes, turning 3 or
4 times to fry evenly. Remove
from oil onto paper towels to
drain. Advise guests to unwrap
very carefully! For a change, substitute chicken for fish.

Yield 20-30 appetizers

Any way you wrap it, it's delish.

9 oz. cream cheese, softened
½ c. soft butter or margarine
1½ c. flour
½ lb. mushrooms, minced
1 large onion, minced
3 T. butter
2 T. flour
1 tsp. salt
¼ tsp. thyme
¼ c. sour cream
1 egg, beaten

Combine cream cheese and ½ cup
butter; work in 1½ cups flour to
form soft dough. Refrigerate for 1
hour. In medium skillet, cook
mushrooms and onion in 3 tablespoons butter for about 5 minutes, over medium heat. Stir in 2
tablespoons flour, salt and
thyme. Add sour cream. Remove
from heat.
    Roll out dough, cut into 3″
circles. Put a teaspoonful of
mushroom mixture on half of
each circle. Brush edges with
beaten egg, fold over, press edges
together with fork. Prick top.
Brush with egg and bake on
ungreased cookie sheet in 450
degree oven for 12-14 minutes.
May be baked ahead, frozen and
reheated.

Yield about 4 dozen

Vietnamese
Egg Roll

Korean
Man Doo Egg Rolls

1 c. chopped and sauteed chicken
  or pork
1 c. chopped crab meat or shrimp
1 c. solidly packed shredded
  carrots
¾ c. finely chopped onion
½ c. thinly sliced jicama or water
  chestnuts
½ c. dried black mushrooms
  (soak until soft, discard stems,
  thinly slice)
salt and pepper
spring roll, Philippine or lumfia
  wrappers
1 egg, beaten
peanut oil for deep frying

Mix first seven ingredients together and chill well for 2-3 hours. Fill wrappers with mixture, roll up, folding ends in and seal with egg. Deep fry a few at a time in hot (350 degrees) oil until brown. Drain on paper towels and serve warm with sweet and sour and/or hot mustard sauce. These can be made ahead and frozen. Reheat in 400 degree oven for 8-10 minutes on bottom shelf.

Yield 8-10 egg rolls

The Vietnamese wrap the egg roll in a lettuce leaf and dip it all into an Oriental fish sauce that has been diluted with sugar, lemon juice, chili sauce and Tabasco to taste.

Spring roll, Philippine or lumfia wrappers are available in Oriental grocery stores.

4 c. vegetable oil
½ lb. lean ground beef
½ lb. lean pork sausage
¼ c. finely chopped green onion
1 c. finely chopped cabbage,
  boiled 1 minute
1 can bean sprouts, drained,
  washed, chopped
1 tsp. sesame oil
¼ tsp. black pepper
2 tsp. salt
1 T. soy sauce
½ T. cornstarch
1 lb. wonton skins (3½" square)

Heat 2 tablespoons oil in wok or frying pan. Brown meats, drain, mix in other ingredients; stir well. Place 1 teaspoon of mixture in center of each wonton skin. Fold skin diagonally, bringing two sides together and rolling up. Brush around edges with water to seal. Heat remaining oil to 350 degrees. Deep fry until skin is golden brown. Remove egg rolls and drain on paper towels.

Yield about 4 dozen

A nice variation on the egg roll theme.

Estonian
Pirukad

Meat-Filled Turnovers

½ c. soft butter or margarine
2 c. flour
1 egg
5 T. sour cream

Filling:
2 c. diced cooked ham
1 medium onion, diced
2 T. butter
salt and pepper to taste
1 egg, lightly beaten

Mix butter, flour, egg and sour cream to form dough. Cover and chill for 1 hour. Saute ham and onion in butter. Add salt and pepper. Divide the dough in half and roll out each half into a thin circle. Cut into 3" rounds. Place a teaspoon of filling near center of each circle and fold over to cover the filling. Brush edges, and top with beaten egg, and seal open edges together. Bake at 350 degrees for 20-25 minutes. Serve warm.

Yield 2 dozen

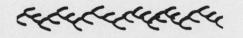

German
Sültze

Jellied Meat

3 lb. pork loin roast
1 tsp. salt
1 large bay leaf
3 c. water
1 c. vinegar
1 T. unflavored gelatin
⅓ c. cold water
salt and pepper to taste
chopped dill pickles (optional)

Place pork, salt, bay leaf and 3 cups of water in large pot. Bring to a boil, cover and reduce to simmer. Cook about 2 hours or until meat is well done. Remove pork, saving liquid, and cut into very small pieces. Strain liquid, cool and remove fat. Bring 2 cups of broth and the vinegar to a boil. Remove from heat and add gelatin which has been dissolved in ⅓ cup cold water. Add meat and season to taste with salt and pepper. Chopped pickles may be added. Pour into 9" x 9" glass dish and chill to congeal. Slice and serve.

10-12 servings

An unusual touch to a cold meat platter.

German
Sauerkraut Balls

1 medium onion, finely chopped
¼ c. butter or margarine
½ c. flour
½ c. water
1 lb. sauerkraut, chopped and drained
1 egg, beaten
½ c. milk
1 c. bread crumbs
shortening for deep frying

In a saucepan, saute onion in butter until soft. Blend ¼ cup of the flour with water and stir into onion. Add sauerkraut and mix well. Cook over low heat, stirring until thick. Cool and shape into 1" balls. Roll in ¼ cup flour. Mix egg and milk and dip balls into mixture, then roll in bread crumbs. Let stand about 15 minutes before deep frying in fat heated to 365 degrees. Fry until golden brown. Drain on paper towels and serve with wooden picks. Can add ½ pound ground ham or corned beef to sauerkraut mixture. These can be reheated in oven and also freeze well.

Yield 3 dozen

An intriguing taste treat.

Greek

Dolmades with Avgolemono Sauce

Stuffed Grape Leaves with Egg and Lemon Sauce

50 fresh grape leaves or 1 jar
   leaves, rinsed in warm water
1 lb. ground beef
1 large onion, finely chopped
¼ c. uncooked rice
1 egg
¼ c. chopped parsley
2 sprigs fresh mint leaves,
   chopped
2 c. hot water (approximately)

Avgolemono Sauce:
3 eggs
juice of 2 lemons (5 to 6 T.)
6 T. liquid from dolmades

Wash fresh grape leaves thoroughly and boil 5 minutes. Mix remaining ingredients except hot water. Place 1 teaspoonful of the filling on the inside (dull side) of each leaf, tuck in ends and roll up. Arrange stuffed leaves very carefully on bottom of heavy pot and layer. Slowly add enough hot water to completely cover dolmades. Invert a plate on top to secure the dolmades; cover and simmer for about 1 hour. Make sauce by beating eggs until thickened. Slowly add lemon juice, beating constantly. Slowly stir liquid from dolmades into egg mixture, 1 tablespoonful at a time so as not to curdle. Pour over dolmades. Allow to stand about 5 minutes before serving.

Yield 4½ dozen

Have small plates and forks ready.

Polish

Chicken Liver Pate

1 lb. chicken livers
¾ c. coarsely chopped onion
½ c. coarsely chopped celery
½ lb. (2 sticks) butter
½ c. brandy
¾ c. chicken broth
1 envelope unflavored gelatin
3 hard-cooked eggs
½ tsp. salt
½ tsp. pepper
¼ tsp. allspice
pinch of nutmeg

Saute chicken livers, onion and celery in butter for 10 minutes over very low heat until livers are cooked but not brown. Add brandy and half of the chicken broth. Dissolve gelatin in remaining half of chicken broth and bring to a gentle simmer. Put celery, onion, chicken livers and hard-cooked eggs in blender (not food processor). Blend until smooth. Add gelatin mixture, salt, pepper, allspice and nutmeg. Mix well. Pour into pate tureen or crock. Chill for 12 hours. Serve with crackers.

12-14 servings

An elegant pate, smooth as velvet!

Jewish
Chopped Liver

Norwegian
Norwegian Meatballs

1 lb. liver (chicken or beef)
4 T. schmaltz, rendered chicken
    fat (see index)
2 medium onions, diced
4 hard-cooked eggs
1½ tsp. salt
¼ tsp. freshly ground pepper
parsley sprigs

Broil or bake liver until tender,
about 3-5 minutes on each side.
Do not overcook as it will tend to
be dry. Rinse with cold water,
peel and devein. Melt 2 tablespoons schmaltz and saute onions
until light brown. Grind onions,
liver and 3 eggs together. Add 2
tablespoons schmaltz or more to
bind and make a smooth mixture.

   Place in mold or on platter and
grate remaining egg over top and
garnish with parsley sprigs. Serve
with crackers or rye bread.

Yield about 1 pound

*In this Jewish pate — schmaltz leads
the way.*

1¼ lb. lean ground beef
¾ lb. ground pork and veal
    combined
2 slices soft white bread without
    crusts
⅔ c. light cream
2 eggs, lightly beaten
1 small onion, grated
2 small or 1 large clove garlic,
    minced
1 T. chopped parsley
1 tsp. salt
¼ tsp. pepper
¼ tsp. nutmeg
¼ tsp. allspice
2 T. margarine
1 T. oil
1½ qt. beef bouillon
¼ c. flour
1 c. water
salt and pepper to taste

Mix together beef, pork and veal
in a large bowl. In separate bowl,
soak bread in cream for a few
minutes, then add to meat. Next
add eggs, onion, garlic, parsley,
salt, pepper, nutmeg and allspice.
Mix thoroughly, using hands, and
shape into 1″ balls; refrigerate for
30 minutes. Heat margarine and
oil in skillet and fry meatballs
until lightly browned. In a large
kettle or Dutch oven, heat the
beef bouillon. Drop browned
meatballs into bouillon and simmer covered for 20 minutes. Mix
flour and water together, add to
broth and simmer 10 minutes
longer. Season to taste with salt
and pepper.

8 servings

*A good reason to use the chafing dish
tucked away in your cupboard.*

Mexican
Guacamole

Avocado Dip

3 ripe avocados
2 T. lemon juice
⅓ c. minced onion
1 tsp. chili powder
3 T. Mexican salsa (see index)

Peel avocados and mash pulp, leaving a few small lumps throughout. Add lemon juice, onion, chili powder and salsa. Mix lightly. If not serving immediately, refrigerate in covered bowl with avocado pits immersed in guacamole to keep avocado from darkening. Serve as a dip with tostadas or corn chips.

Yield about 2 cups

Classic Mexican dip!

Middle Eastern
Humus and Techina

Chick Pea Spread

1 (15½ oz.) can garbanzo beans
juice of 1 lemon (2 T.)
1 small clove garlic, peeled
2 T. olive oil
3 T. Techina (see index) or plain
    Tahin from jar

Drain beans. Blend with lemon juice, garlic, olive oil and techina in blender, food processor or thoroughly mash by hand, until smooth. Spread in mound on flat plate and swirl with knife to flatten. Drizzle a little olive oil over the top, if desired. Serve at room temperature with Pita Bread (see index).

Yield 2 cups

To create a true mideastern atmosphere, Humus is a must.

Greek
Feta Cheese Pie

¾ lb. Feta cheese
5 eggs, well beaten
1 tsp. salt
pepper
several drops of Tabasco
10 sheets of phyllo (filo) dough
melted butter

Mash Feta cheese; mix together with eggs, salt, pepper and Tabasco. Place 3 sheets of phyllo dough, cut to fit, in 9″ x 13″ greased pan, brushing each sheet with melted butter. Keep additional sheets covered with damp towel to prevent drying. Pour in ⅓ of cheese mixture, then 2 sheets of phyllo, alternating layers, finishing with 3 sheets of phyllo dough, brushing with melted butter between each sheet. Bake at 350 degrees for 30-35 minutes or until light brown and crisp. Cut in squares and serve.

12-14 servings

Phyllo (filo) pastry leaves or sheets, often referred to as strudel dough, may be found frozen in 1 pound packages of 20-25 sheets, 16″ x 18″ in measurement. Thaw overnight in refrigerator. The leaves keep in refrigerator for about 10 days and unused portions must be covered with a damp cloth, as they dry out quickly. They may be kept frozen up to a year and can be refrozen.

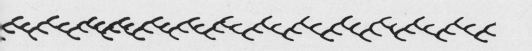

Jewish
Bailik

Mock Gefilte Fish Balls

4 chicken breasts (2½-3 c.
   chicken) ground
1 medium onion
1 carrot
2 eggs
¼ tsp. sugar
2 tsp. salt
1/8 tsp. pepper
2 T. matzo meal or bread crumbs
1 qt. water
½ tsp. sugar
2 tsp. salt
2 large onions, diced

Grind chicken, 1 onion and carrot
together. Add eggs, ¼ teaspoon
sugar, 2 teaspoons salt and pepper, then matzo meal; mix thoroughly. Let stand for ½ hour;
shape into 1½"-2" balls. Bring
water to a boil with ½ teaspoon
sugar, 2 teaspoons salt and diced
onions. Add balls to boiling water
and let boil for 1 hour. Lift out
with a slotted spoon. Serve at
room temperature or cold with
Horseradish (see index).

Yield 16-18 balls

*You can make them tiny and serve on
picks.*

Jewish
Gefilte Fish

10 lb. any combination fish (pike,
   walleye, pickerel, white fish or
   buffalo fish, including head and
   bones)
3 large onions
1 carrot, sliced
¼ tsp. pepper
2 T. salt
6 eggs
1 c. matzo meal or bread crumbs
2 c. water plus 1 tsp. sugar

Fillet fish and grind, or chop in
wooden bowl, with 1 onion. Put
washed bones and heads in a large
soup pot; barely cover with
water; add 1 onion, carrot, dash
of pepper and 1 tablespoon salt;
cover and let simmer while pre-
paring fish balls.

Combine fish, 1 chopped
onion, eggs, matzo meal, 1 tablespoon salt, pepper and sugar
water in a bowl. Beat mixture
with an electric mixer at least 10
minutes. Using ice cream scoop or
wet hands, make balls and place
in stock. Cook covered until fish
turns white, about 3 hours. When
cooked, remove with slotted
spoon and place on a plate and
garnish with carrots. Serve cold
with Horseradish (see index).

Yield 25 pieces

*Grandma would have loved having a
food processor for this one — if you
have one use it.*

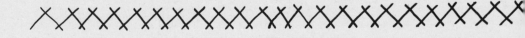

Italian
Wedding Soup

2 eggs
¼ c. bread crumbs
¼ c. grated Romano cheese
lemon rind to taste
pinch of nutmeg
3 c. chicken broth
parsley

Mix first five ingredients. Let stand a few minutes. Drop by teaspoonfuls into boiling chicken broth and simmer until done. Garnish with parsley. This recipe makes 2 servings; just multiply as needed.

   For variety, make your own favorite meatball recipe. Form into balls about the size of marbles. When egg drop is done, add meatballs to broth and cook a few minutes.

2 servings

Don't wait for a wedding to try this one, it's good for anniversaries, too.

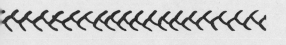

Jewish
Chicken Soup

4-5 lb. stewing or roasting
   chicken, cut up
1 large onion, peeled
4 stalks celery, cut into 1" pieces
4 carrots, cut into 1" pieces
1 parsnip, cut into 1" pieces
2 tsp. salt
1 tsp. dill weed (optional)
1 tsp. minced fresh parsley
freshly ground pepper
½ tsp. sugar (optional)

Place chicken pieces in large soup kettle, cover with cold water. Bring to a boil; immediately reduce heat and skim off top. Add vegetables and seasonings. Cover and simmer 2-2½ hours or until chicken is very tender. Remove chicken and vegetables. Strain broth into large container and chill until fat rises to top for easy removal. If chicken is to be served in the soup, remove meat from bones, cut into small pieces and add to the broth before reheating.

   To serve, reheat soup and add cooked rice, Noodles or Matzo Balls (see index).

Yield approximately 3 quarts

Rx: "Jewish penicillin"

Czechoslovakian
Kureci Polévka

South Bohemian Chicken Soup

½ c. dried black mushrooms
2½-3 lb. chicken, cut up
4½ c. water
1 large potato, peeled and diced
½ c. diced celery
½ c. diced carrots
2 T. butter
1 (8 oz.) can peas, drained
1 clove garlic, mashed with ½
   tsp. salt
2 tsp. marjoram
1 T. flour
½ c. cream
salt to taste

Cover mushrooms with water and let soak until soft. Simmer chicken in 4½ cups water with potato, celery and carrots. Drain mushrooms; slice and saute in butter with peas. When chicken is tender, remove from stock; take meat from bones and return chicken to stock. Add mushrooms and peas and simmer covered. Add garlic with salt and marjoram to the soup. Blend flour with cream and pour into pot, season with salt, stirring constantly. Simmer 10-12 minutes. Serve with dark rye bread.

4 servings

Add a salad and your dinner's done!

German
Green Bean Soup

1 meaty ham bone
2 qt. water
1 large onion, chopped
2-3 c. green beans, cut into 1"
  pieces
4 large carrots, sliced
4 large potatoes, peeled and diced
  (new potatoes, with skins left
  on, may also be used)
1 pt. whipping cream
salt and pepper
fresh parsley, finely chopped

Cover ham bone with water in a
large kettle. Add onion and bring
to a boil. Cover and simmer until
meat is very tender, 2-3 hours.
Remove meat from bone and cut
into bite-size pieces. Degrease
stock; return bone to stock, adding water if necessary. Add green
beans, carrots and potatoes. Simmer 20-30 minutes or until vegetables are tender. Add meat to soup
and remove bone; stir in cream;
heat soup thoroughly. Season to
taste with salt and pepper. Garnish with parsley.

6-8 servings

Italian
Fagioli

Bean and Macaroni Soup

¼ c. vegetable oil
½ onion, chopped
1 clove garlic, minced
2 (6 oz.) cans tomato paste
6 cans water
1 (15 oz.) can kidney beans
¼ tsp. salt
¼ tsp. pepper
6 qt. water
1 T. salt
1 lb. ditali pasta (elbow
  macaroni)
½ c. grated Parmesan cheese

In saucepan, heat oil, add onion
and garlic and saute until lightly
browned. Add tomato paste and
water; blend well. Add beans, ¼
teaspoon salt and pepper. Simmer
for 45 minutes.

Bring 6 quarts water and 1
tablespoon salt to a boil. Add
pasta and cook about 12 minutes
or until pasta is *al dente* (firm to
the bite); drain, leaving about ¾
cup cooking water in pasta. To
this, add sauce and let stand covered about 10 minutes. Sprinkle
with cheese and serve.

6 servings

Greek
Faki Soupa

Lentil Soup

1 lb. lentils
2 medium onions, chopped
3 stalks celery, chopped
2 small carrots, chopped
2 cloves garlic, minced
1 T. tomato sauce
2 bay leaves
1 tsp. oregano
olive oil
½ c. red wine or vinegar
salt and pepper

Rinse and drain lentils. Saute next
four ingredients in olive oil in a
heavy soup pot. Add tomato
sauce, bay leaves, oregano and
lentils with enough water to cover; stir, bring to boil, reduce heat
and simmer covered for about 45
minutes. Check periodically to
see that the water covers the lentils, adding more if necessary.
When lentils are tender, add wine
and salt and pepper to taste.

Yield about 10 cups

Traditionally served during Lent.

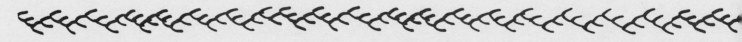

German
Lentil Soup

1 c. lentils
4½ c. water
1½ tsp. salt
½ tsp. pepper
3 (or more) Polish sausage links,
   cut into small pieces
1½ c. coarsely chopped onions

Bring lentils and water to a boil,
reduce heat and simmer covered
½ hour. Add salt, pepper, sausage and onion and cook until
onion is tender, about 1 hour.

4-6 servings

*This soup was a specialty served with
popovers at the original Schiek's
restaurant in downtown
Minneapolis.*

Swedish
Gul Artsoppa

Yellow Pea Soup

1¾-2 c. whole dried yellow peas
2 qt. water
1 lb. pork shoulder or 1 meaty
   ham bone
2 medium onions, chopped
2-3 carrots, sliced
1 tsp. salt (more to taste if
   desired)
½ tsp. freshly ground pepper
1 tsp. crumbled dried marjoram

Wash peas. Place in soup kettle,
add water and bring to a brisk
boil for 3 minutes. Remove from
heat, cover and soak for 1 hour.
Discard any pea husks that float
to surface. Add meat, bring to a
boil, skim and add vegetables and
seasonings. Simmer covered 1½-
2 hours or until peas are tender
but not mushy.
   Serve soup with a few pieces of
meat, Swedish rye bread, butter
and dark brown mustard.

4-6 servings

*Pureeing the peas after cooking will
give you a smoother soup.*

Finnish
Kalakeitto

Fish and Vegetable Soup

3 medium potatoes, peeled and
   diced
2 large carrots, sliced
1 medium onion, diced
2 c. chicken broth
1 c. dry white wine
1 lb. lean fish fillets (northern,
   walleye or white fish), cut up
2 large tomatoes, peeled and
   diced (or ½-1 c. canned)
1 tsp. fresh chopped dill weed (or
   ½ tsp. dried)
½ tsp. salt
3 green onions, chopped,
   including green tops

In a large saucepan, add potatoes,
carrots and onion to broth and
wine. Bring to boil, cover; simmer until vegetables are tender.
Add fish, tomatoes, dill weed and
salt. Simmer until fish flakes with
fork. Serve topped with chopped
green onion.

4-5 servings

You'll "finnish" every drop!

Russian

Krupnik

Vegetable and Barley Soup

½ lb. chick peas (garbanzos)
½ lb. large lima beans
½ lb. lentils
1 lb. soup meat, cut into 1" cubes
2 or 3 marrow bones
3 carrots, cut in pieces
8 c. water
½ lb. barley
salt to taste

Wash and soak chick peas and lima beans in cold water overnight, or bring to a boil and let soak for 1 hour. Rinse lentils in colander. In a large pot, place chick peas, beans (including water in which they were soaked), lentils, meat, marrow bones, carrots and 8 cups water. Bring to gentle boil. Reduce heat and simmer covered 1½ hours or until meat is tender. Cook barley with salt separately according to package directions. Add to soup and simmer about ½ hour longer, adding more water if necessary.

12 servings

Italian

Florentine Soup

1 (10 oz.) pkg. frozen chopped spinach
1 c. canned cannellini beans
2 cans chicken broth
¼ tsp. thyme
¼ tsp. dill weed
1 bay leaf
2 egg yolks
juice of 1 medium lemon (2 T.)
1 c. cooked rice
grated Parmesan cheese

Cook spinach as directed on package; do not drain. Puree cannellini beans with liquid and one can of chicken broth in blender or food processor. In a large pot add the second can of broth, spices, spinach and bean mixture. Bring to boil and simmer 30 minutes. Beat egg yolks with lemon juice and add slowly to the simmering soup, stirring constantly. Do not boil. Add rice. Serve hot or cold with grated Parmesan cheese sprinkled on top.

6 servings

Polish

Zupa Kartoflana

Potato Soup

3 medium potatoes, peeled and sliced
1 large onion, thinly sliced
2 stalks celery, cut in 1" pieces
2 carrots, cut in 1" pieces
2 qt. water
salt and pepper
3 T. butter
1 T. flour
1 c. half-and-half cream, heated
1 sprig parsley, chopped

Cover all vegetables with water; add salt and pepper to taste. Cover and cook until well done. Force through sieve. Heat butter until light brown, stir in flour and let mixture cook until it bubbles and is well blended. Gradually add hot cream to flour mixture and let simmer just below boiling point until mixture is smooth and thick. Add to strained vegetables and let simmer until thick. Sprinkle with chopped parsley.

6-8 servings

To thaw the Minnesota "chill-nik."

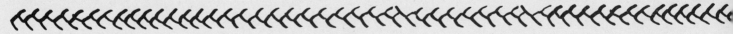

Welsh

Leek and Potato Soup

3 leeks
4 medium potatoes
4 T. butter or margarine
2 qt. chicken stock
2 T. flour
1 c. milk
salt and pepper
3 sprigs parsley, minced

Trim leeks, wash thoroughly and thinly slice. Peel and dice potatoes. Melt 2 tablespoons butter in a 3-4 quart saucepan. Add leeks and potatoes. Cover and cook over medium heat until the leeks are lightly colored, about 5 minutes. Shake pan gently or stir carefully to prevent the vegetables from burning. Add chicken stock. Increase heat, then reduce to simmer; cover and cook 45 minutes.

In a small saucepan, melt the remaining 2 tablespoons of butter, stir in flour, using a wooden spoon. Slowly stir in milk, making sure there are no lumps. Cook 2-3 minutes over low heat; when thickened, stir into soup. Season to taste with salt and pepper. Garnish each serving with parsley.

8-10 servings

Puree, chill and it's almost Vichyssoise.

Swedish

Doppa Gryta

Hearty Soup

2-4 lb. beef rump roast
2-4 lb. lean pork roast
water
2 bay leaves
8 peppercorns
2 tsp. salt
2-3 potato sausages
1-2 loaves unsliced "2 day old" bread

Brown roasts well under broiler, drain off fat. Place in large soup kettle, cover with water; add seasonings. Cover and slowly simmer 2-3 hours or until meat is completely tender. Add potato sausages, simmer covered another 30 minutes. As sausages simmer, pierce casings to release juices into the soup. When ready to serve, remove bay leaves and ladle soup broth into bowls. Offer thick slices of bread to dip into the savory broth. The meat is usually sliced and served on the side.

16-20 servings

In Swedish tradition, this is served on Christmas Eve. The gentry join the servants in the kitchen and together dip their chunks of bread into the soup, signifying the common unity of man.

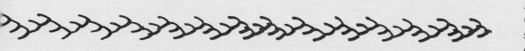

Polish

Borscht

Hot Beef and Beet Soup

3-4 lb. beef ribs
5 c. boiling water
salt and pepper
fresh parsley, dill, chervil,
    chopped
12 beets, washed, peeled and cut
    in strips
2-3 potatoes, cubed
3-4 carrots, diced
2 c. tomato juice
sour cream

Add meat to water and simmer
until nearly tender. Skim off fat.
Season with salt, pepper and
herbs to taste. Add vegetables;
cover and simmer until tender.
Stir in tomato juice. Simmer for
2-3 hours. Remove ribs. For a
hearty dish, cut meat from bones
and return to soup. Serve with a
dollop of sour cream and Polish
rye bread and butter.

10-12 servings

Danish

Cold Cucumber Soup

3 cucumbers, peeled
2 T. butter
1 leek, or 2-3 green onions, sliced
    (use white part only)
1 bay leaf
1 T. flour
3 c. chicken stock
1 tsp. salt
1 c. heavy cream
juice of ½ lemon (1 T.)
1 tsp. finely chopped fresh mint
salt and pepper
½ c. sour cream or yogurt

Cube 2 of the cucumbers. Saute in
butter with leek and bay leaf.
Continue to cook until tender but
not brown, about 20 minutes. Stir
in flour. Add chicken stock and
salt; simmer for 30 minutes. Put
mixture through food mill or
blend half at a time in blender or
food processor. Strain and chill.
Remove seeds and grate remaining cucumber. Add to soup with
cream and lemon juice. Stir in
mint; salt and pepper to taste.
Chill at least 30 minutes more.
Serve in chilled cups topped with
sour cream or yogurt.

6 servings

Cool as a cucumber.

Russian

Beet Borscht

Cold Soup

1 bunch fresh beets with tops
2 large onions, thinly sliced
2 T. salt
½ c. sugar
juice of 3 lemons
6 eggs, beaten
1 pt. sour cream

Scrape, clean and grate beets.
Wash and cut up leaves. In large
kettle, place beets, leaves and
sliced onions. Add water to cover
ingredients and bring to a boil;
skim. Add salt, sugar and lemon
juice to boiling beets. Gradually
add ½ cup hot borscht to beaten
eggs; combine this mixture with
remaining borscht. Mix in sour
cream, a little at a time. Stir well.
Chill and serve icy cold with fresh
dark bread and butter.

Yield 5 quarts

*On a hot summer day this can't be
"beet."*

Spanish
Gazpacho

Cold Tomato Soup

½ medium green pepper,
    chopped
6 large tomatoes, peeled and
    chopped
2 onions, chopped
1 cucumber, peeled and chopped
1 clove garlic, crushed
1½ c. tomato juice
¼ c. olive or vegetable oil
3 T. red wine vinegar
½ tsp. salt
¼ tsp. pepper
dash of Tabasco
fresh chopped parsley or chives
    for garnish

Combine first eight ingredients in
blender or food processor and
puree or, if desired, combine
chopped vegetables with tomato
juice for a chunkier version. Season with salt, pepper and Tabasco. Refrigerate until very cold.
Serve in chilled bowls and sprinkle with chopped parsley.

6-10 servings

*There are many different
consistencies for gazpacho — chop to
your choosing.*

Polish
Cauliflower Soup

1 medium head cauliflower
2 T. butter
2 T. flour
4 c. vegetable or meat stock
salt and pepper
2 egg yolks
¼ c. half and half cream
1 (4 oz.) can mushroom pieces,
    sauteed in 2 T. butter
1 T. dill weed
sour cream (optional)
croutons

Cook cauliflower in salted water
until tender, about 15-20 minutes.
Reserve 3-6 flowerets; drain and
mash remaining cauliflower. Melt
butter and stir in flour, keeping it
light colored. Add slowly to the
vegetable stock in a large pot; salt
and pepper to taste and simmer a
few minutes. Beat egg yolks with
light cream and gradually add to
soup, stirring constantly to avoid
curdling. Add the whole flowerets
and mushrooms; heat through.
Top each serving with a sprinkle
of dill weed and 1 teaspoon sour
cream. Serve with croutons.

6 servings

Chinese
Hot Sour Soup

6 oz. lean pork or chicken, sliced
    against the grain into very thin
    1″ strips
2 tsp. cornstarch
2 tsp. soy sauce
½ tsp. sugar
4 c. chicken broth
6 black mushrooms, soaked in
    warm water, stems discarded
    and cut into thin strips
2 tsp. white pepper or to taste
2 T. vinegar
½ tsp. salt
1 T. cornstarch dissolved in 3 T.
    water
1 egg, beaten
1 tsp. sesame oil
2 T. finely chopped green onion

Mix meat with cornstarch, soy
sauce and sugar; set aside to marinate. In a large pot, combine
chicken broth and mushroom
strips. Bring to a boil over high
heat. Add meat, and while stirring, bring to a second boil. Add
pepper, vinegar and salt. Boil
about 1½ minutes. Add dissolved
cornstarch and stir until slightly
thickened. *Very slowly* pour in
beaten egg, stirring constantly.
Add sesame oil, stir well and
serve immediately. Garnish each
serving with green onion.

4 servings

Finnish

Sekahedelmäkeitto

Fruit Soup

1 (16 oz.) pkg. pitted dried prunes
1 (8 oz.) pkg. dried apricots
1 (6 oz.) can frozen orange juice
   concentrate
5 c. water
rind of 1 lemon, pared very thinly
2 T. quick tapioca
1 - 3" stick cinnamon
½ c. sugar
¼ c. sour cream
¼ c. grated orange rind

Combine prunes, apricots, orange juice and water in a large saucepan. Let stand ½ hour. Add lemon rind, tapioca, cinnamon and sugar. Simmer covered for 10 minutes. Remove cinnamon stick and lemon peel; cool. Serve in individual glass bowls; garnish with sour cream and orange rind.

6 servings

Served throughout Scandinavia as a first course, dessert or even for breakfast.

Japanese

Egg Flower Suimono

Clear Soup

6 c. chicken or pork stock
1 tsp. salt
¾ c. coarsely chopped cooked
   pork or chicken breast
½ c. minced onion
½ c. sliced water chestnuts
½ c. sliced mushrooms
½ c. sliced bamboo shoots
few drops soy sauce

Egg Flower Batter:
1 tsp. cornstarch
2 eggs
1 T. cold water

Combine stock, salt, cooked meat, onion, water chestnuts, mushrooms, bamboo shoots and soy sauce and bring to a boil. Simmer covered for 30 minutes. Mix egg flower batter. Gradually trickle batter into simmering soup with a slotted spoon. The egg batter will float to the top.

6-8 servings

Delightfully delicate.

New England

Clam Chowder

2 (7-8-oz.) cans clams or 2-3 doz.
   fresh steamed clams
¼ lb. salt pork, diced
1 qt. water
2 large potatoes, pared and diced
2 onions, minced
2 c. milk
1 T. butter
salt and pepper to taste
oyster crackers (optional)

Drain clams, reserving liquid. In large saucepan, fry salt pork until crisp. Remove pork and reserve. Add water, reserved clam liquid, potatoes and onions to fat in saucepan. Cook covered until potatoes are tender, about 15-20 minutes. Add milk, butter and seasonings. Add clams either cut, minced or whole and only cook about 3 minutes as long cooking makes the clams tough. Top each serving with pork pieces and oyster crackers if desired.

6 servings

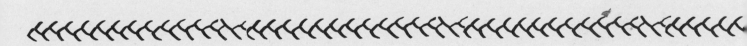

Vietnamese
Cream of Crab Soup

1 medium onion, chopped
2 tsp. butter
½ lb. crab meat, fresh, frozen or
  canned
6 c. chicken broth
1-2 (17 oz.) cans creamed corn
salt and pepper

Place onion in kettle with butter
and saute until brown. Add crab-
meat, which has been rinsed and
picked over, and stir-fry a minute
or two. Add chicken broth and
bring to a boil. Stir in corn, salt
and pepper to taste. Serve hot.

Yield 2 quarts

The cream of the crab.

Minnesota
Wild Rice Soup

1 medium onion, thinly sliced
4 oz. fresh mushrooms, sliced or
  chopped
3 T. butter
¼ c. flour
4 c. chicken stock
1½ c. cooked wild rice
1 c. half-and-half cream
¼ c. dry sherry
chopped parsley

Cut sliced onion into quarters.
Cook onion and mushrooms in
butter until onion is transparent.
Add flour and cook for 15 minutes, stirring occasionally. Add
chicken stock and cook approximately 10 minutes, stirring until
smooth. Add wild rice, cream and
sherry, stirring until heated
throughout. Garnish with
parsley.

6-8 servings

*A marvelous soup made from our
precious homegrown harvest.*

Hungarian
Hungarian Goulash Soup

1 lb. lean boneless beef (shank or
  chuck), diced in ¼" cubes
2 large yellow onions, finely diced
1 T. paprika
2 T. tomato puree
2 cloves garlic, crushed
1 T. salt
1 tsp. black pepper
2 T. flour
2 qt. beef stock (made from beef
  bones) or water
3 medium red potatoes, diced
½ tsp. caraway seed
1 strip very thin lemon peel
butter

Brown meat in heavy saucepan or
stew pot, add onions, paprika,
tomato puree, garlic, salt and
pepper. Mix well. Dust with flour
and add beef stock. Bring to boil,
stirring occasionally and let simmer covered for 1 hour. Add
potatoes and continue cooking
until both meat and potatoes are
done. Chop caraway seeds and
lemon peel very finely with small
amount of butter and add to soup
about 10 minutes before serving.

8-10 servings

American

Turkey Soup

1 (12-16 lb.) turkey carcass
1-2 bay leaves
5-6 whole cloves
salt and pepper to taste
2 T. butter
3 T. flour
2 T. chicken base
½ c. uncooked rice
¼ c. chopped onion
1 c. chopped celery
1 c. leftover gravy and turkey
   dressing
¼ tsp. curry powder (optional)
1 hard cooked egg, minced
½ c. orange juice
½ c. Port wine
6-8 orange slices

Cut meat from bones, and cover carcass with water. Add bay leaves, cloves, salt and pepper.

Simmer for 3-4 hours. Remove bones and drain stock through a colander. Make a roux by melting the butter and adding flour and chicken base. Add this to the drained liquid a little at a time. Bring to a boil, using a wire whisk to blend thoroughly. Add rice, onion, celery and season to taste. Cook about 25 minutes until rice is done. Add diced turkey and about 1 cup of the leftover gravy and turkey dressing. If using curry, mix it with a little broth and add to the soup. Simmer until serving. Add minced egg, orange juice and wine just before serving and top bowls with orange slices.

6-8 servings

South American

Sopa De Zapallo

Cold Pumpkin Soup

1 onion, diced
6 scallions, bulbs and greens
   sliced separately
5 c. chicken broth
2½ c. pumpkin puree, canned or
   fresh
salt and cayenne pepper
2 c. light cream
2 tomatoes, thinly sliced
1 c. heavy cream, whipped

Cook onion and bulb portion of scallions in chicken broth until soft, about 15 minutes. Puree through a sieve and return to broth. Stir in pumpkin puree and simmer for 10 to 15 minutes until thick and smooth. Season with salt and pepper and chill well. Just before serving, stir in 2 cups light cream and adjust seasoning. Serve in cups with 2 slices of tomato, a dab of whipped cream and a sprinkling of sliced green scallion tops.

6-8 servings

the staff of life

English
English Rye Bread

American
Tomato Quick Bread

1 pkg. dry yeast
¼ c. warm water (105-115 degrees)
1 tsp. sugar
¼ c. shortening
2½ c. warm water
½ c. dark molasses
1 T. salt
3 c. rye flour
4 c. white flour

Dissolve yeast in ¼ cup warm water with sugar. Melt shortening, add 2½ cups warm water, molasses, salt and dissolved yeast. Add rye flour. Mix well, then add white flour gradually to make a soft dough. Knead on floured board and place in greased bowl, cover and let rise until double. Punch down. Let rise again. Shape into 2 loaves; put in 8½" x 4½" greased loaf pans. Let rise until over top of pan. Bake in 375 degree oven for 30-35 minutes or until golden brown. Remove from pans immediately and cool on rack.

Yield 2 loaves

Extremely delicious!

2½ c. flour
1 T. baking powder
1 tsp. salt
1 tsp. garlic salt
1 tsp. crushed oregano
1 T. sugar
½ c. shredded Mozzarella cheese
¼ c. grated Parmesan cheese
⅓-⅔ c. milk
1½ c. peeled, chopped tomatoes, drained (reserve liquid)
2 eggs
¼ c. vegetable oil

Stir together flour, baking powder, salts, oregano, sugar and cheeses. Add enough milk to drained tomato liquid to make ⅔ cup. Blend liquid with eggs and oil. Stir liquid and chopped tomatoes into flour mixture; mix thoroughly. Pour batter into greased 8½" x 4½" loaf pan. Bake at 350 degrees for 75-80 minutes.

Yield 1 loaf

A good recipe for tomatoes left over from the garden.

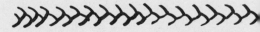

Swedish
Swedish Rye Bread

2 pkg. dry yeast
1½ c. warm water (105-115 degrees)
¼ c. molasses
⅓ c. sugar
1 T. salt
2 T. shortening
3-4 T. grated orange rind or 1 tsp. anise seed
2½ c. medium rye flour
2¼-2¾ c. white flour
3-4 T. cornmeal

Dissolve yeast in warm water in large mixing bowl. Stir in molasses, sugar, salt, shortening and orange rind. Mix in rye flour until smooth. Stir in white flour with hands until thoroughly blended. Turn onto lightly floured board. Cover and let rest 10-15 minutes. Knead until smooth. Place in greased bowl. Turn greased side up. Cover, let rise until double, about 1 hour. Punch down dough and make one round. Cover and let rise again until double, about 40 minutes.

Punch down. Divide dough into 2 parts and shape into 2 round, slightly flattened loaves. Grease a cookie sheet and sprinkle with cornmeal. Place loaves on opposite corners of the cookie sheet. Cover and let rise 1 hour. Bake 30-35 minutes at 375 degrees.

Yield 2 round loaves

American
Cracked Wheat Bread

2 c. boiling water
2 c. cracked wheat
½ c. brown sugar or honey
2 T. butter
1 T. salt
2 pkg. dry yeast
½ c. warm water (105-115 degrees)
5-5½ c. flour

Combine boiling water, cracked wheat, brown sugar, butter and salt in a large mixing bowl. Cool to warm. Meanwhile, soften yeast in warm water. Combine both mixtures. Beat in 4 cups flour. Turn out onto floured surface and knead in enough of remaining flour to make a moderately stiff dough. Knead 10 minutes. Place in greased bowl and cover. Let rise in a warm place until double, about 1½ hours. Punch down and shape into 2 loaves. Place in greased 8½" x 4½" loaf pans, turning to grease all surfaces. Let rise until double, about 1½ hours. Bake at 350 degrees for 30 minutes.

Yield 2 loaves

This marvelous bread, served at the Minnetonka Arts Center, is a winner.

American
Date Nut Bread

1 tsp. baking soda
1 c. dates, cut-up
½ c. raisins
grated rind of 1 orange
1 c. boiling water
1 T. orange juice
¼ lb. soft butter or margarine
1 c. sugar
2 eggs
1 tsp. vanilla
2 c. flour
¼ c. nuts

Sprinkle baking soda over dates, raisins and orange rind. Add water and orange juice and set aside. Cream butter and sugar. Add eggs, one at a time, and then vanilla. Add flour, alternating with liquid from date-raisin mixture, until both flour and liquid are used up. Dust nuts with 1 tablespoon flour and fold into batter. Fold in fruits. Pour into 4 well greased 16 ounce cans or two 8" loaf pans. Fill ⅔ full. Bake at 350 degrees for 1 hour.

Yield 4 round or 2 oblong loaves

American
Brown Sugar Nut Bread

2 c. flour
2½ tsp. baking powder
½ tsp. salt
1 c. brown sugar
1 c. milk
1 c. coarsely chopped nuts
1 c. seedless raisins or chopped dates

In a bowl, combine flour, baking powder, salt, and brown sugar. Mix well. Stir in milk, nuts, and raisins. Pour batter into greased 5" x 9" loaf pan or two 3½" x 7½" pans. Bake at 325 degrees for 1¼ hours for large loaf or one hour for two small loaves; or until a wooden pick inserted in center comes out clean. When loaves are done turn out onto a rack to cool.

Yield one large or two small loaves

Finnish
Cardamom Bread

¼ c. butter
2½ c. milk, scalded
2 pkg. dry yeast
2½ c. flour
2 eggs, beaten
¾ c. sugar
1 tsp. salt
1 tsp. ground cardamom
4 c. flour

Glaze:
½ c. powdered sugar
¼ c. half-and-half cream, milk or strong coffee

Put butter into scalded milk; cool to lukewarm (105-115 degrees) and stir in the yeast. Add flour and beat until batter is smooth. Let stand ½ hour or until bubble action starts. Beat in eggs, sugar, salt, and cardamom. Blend in approximately four cups of flour. Knead thoroughly; let rise until double. Make two braids or shape as desired and place on greased cookie sheets. Let rise until triple. Bake at 350 degrees for 45 minutes. Mix glaze and pour over breads while still warm. This dough could also be used for cinnamon rolls.

Yield 2 loaves

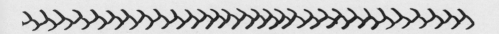

Norwegian
Cardamom Rolls

2 c. milk, scalded
2 pkg. dry yeast
½ c. soft margarine
1 c. sugar
3 eggs
1 tsp. ground cardamom
7 c. flour
melted butter or egg white
chopped almonds

Cool milk until lukewarm (105-115 degrees). Sprinkle yeast on top of milk. Let stand for 10 minutes; do not stir. In a bowl, cream margarine and sugar. Add eggs, one at a time. Stir yeast and milk and add cardamom. Combine with egg mixture, then stir in flour. Knead dough until smooth. Place in greased large bowl and let rise until double. Punch down and let rise again until double. Divide dough and shape into dinner size rolls. Place in two 9" x 12" pans and let rise again until double. Brush tops with butter or egg white; sprinkle with chopped almonds. Bake at 375 degrees for 15-18 minutes.

Yield about 3 dozen

Jewish
Cheese Rolls

2 pkg. dry yeast
2 c. warm milk (105-115 degrees)
1 tsp. sugar
3 eggs
1 c. sugar
1 tsp. salt
½ c. soft butter
6 c. flour

Filling:
1½ lb. farmer cheese (dry cottage cheese)
3 eggs
1 T. sugar
salt to taste
2 T. melted butter
1 egg, beaten
cinnamon-sugar

Dissolve yeast in warm milk; add 1 teaspoon sugar and let stand for 10 minutes. Beat eggs, 1 cup sugar, salt and butter in large bowl of electric mixer until light. Add flour alternately with yeast-milk-sugar mixture; beat 10 minutes.

Place in large greased bowl, cover with foil and refrigerate overnight. Next morning, let dough rise in warm place for 2 hours before handling.

Make cheese filling by pressing cheese through a colander or sieve. Beat eggs, add to cheese; add sugar and salt to taste. Mix until thick and creamy.

Divide dough into 4 parts, adding flour if needed to roll out. On floured board, roll each part into a rectangle about ⅓" thick. Brush with melted butter and spread with ¼ of the cheese mixture. Roll up like a jelly roll and place on greased cookie sheet. Cover and let rise until double. Before baking, brush rolls with beaten egg and sprinkle with cinnamon-sugar. Bake in 350 degree oven for 25-30 minutes.

Yield 4 long loaves

English
English Muffins

1 pkg. dry yeast dissolved in ¼ c. warm water (105-115 degrees)
½ c. lukewarm milk
½ c. lukewarm water
3 T. melted shortening
1½ tsp. salt
1 T. sugar
1 egg, beaten
4 c. sifted flour (approximately)
½ c. cornmeal

Add dissolved yeast to lukewarm milk and water; then add all other ingredients except cornmeal, forming a medium dough. Turn out onto a well-floured pastry cloth and knead several minutes until smooth, adding more flour if necessary. Place in a greased bowl, cover and let stand until double. When double, roll about ½" thick, let rest about two minutes, then cut with a 4" round cutter. Place muffins on a cornmeal-sprinkled cookie sheet and let rise about 30 minutes. Bake on ungreased griddle about seven minutes on each side.

Yield about 1 dozen

Split and serve toasted with butter and marmalade.

French
Croissants

1½ c. soft butter or margarine
⅓ c. flour
2 pkg. dry yeast
½ c. warm water (105-115 degrees)
¾ c. milk
¼ c. sugar
1 tsp. salt
1 egg
3¾-4¼ c. flour
1 egg yolk
1 T. milk

Cream butter with ⅓ cup flour. Roll mixture between waxed paper to 6" x 12" rectangle. Chill 1 hour or longer. Soften yeast in warm water. Heat ¾ cup milk, sugar and salt until sugar dissolves. Cool to lukewarm. Add softened yeast and 1 egg; beat well. Stir in 2 cups of the flour; beat well. Stir in enough remaining flour to make a moderately soft dough. Knead on floured surface until smooth and elastic, 8-10 minutes.

Roll to 14" square. Place chilled butter on one half; fold over other half and seal edges. Roll to 12" x 21" rectangle. Fold in thirds. (If butter softens, chill after each rolling.) Roll to 12" x 21" rectangle. Fold and roll twice more; seal edges. Fold in thirds to 7" x 12". Chill 45 minutes. Cut dough crosswise in fourths. Roll each fourth to 7" x 20" rectangle. Cut each in 10 pie-shaped wedges, 4" at base and 7" long. Roll loosely from base toward point.

Place on ungreased cookie sheets, point down; curve ends. Cover, let rise until double, 30-45 minutes. Beat egg yolk with 1 tablespoon milk; brush on rolls. Bake at 375 degrees for 12-15 minutes. Remove from sheets; cool.

Yield about 3½ dozen

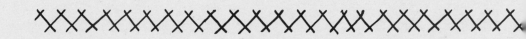

Egyptian
Baladi Bread

1 pkg. dry yeast
1 T. sugar
1-1/8 c. warm water (105-115 degrees)
3 c. flour
1 tsp. salt
¼ c. sesame seeds

Dissolve yeast and sugar in 1/8 cup warm water. Sift flour and salt together. Mix flour with 1 cup warm water. Add yeast to the flour mixture and knead well; the dough should be smooth and firm. If necessary, add a little water or flour to get proper consistency. Cover dough and let rise until double, 2-3 hours.

Divide dough into 8 or 10 pieces, shape each piece into a ball, pat down, sprinkle sesame seeds on top and roll to about ¼" thick. Place on ungreased cookie sheets, four to a sheet, and let stand, covered with a towel, for 1 hour. Bake in 500 degree oven for 5-7 minutes or until the top is lightly browned. The bread will puff up while baking and collapse when cool.

Yield 8-10

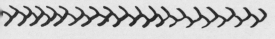

Jewish
Challah

Sabbath Twist

1 tsp. salt
¼ c. sugar
¼ c. vegetable oil
1/8 tsp. saffron (optional)
1¼ c. hot tap water (115-120 degrees)
1 pkg. dry yeast
2 eggs
5 c. flour
1 egg yolk, combined with 1 T. water
sesame or poppy seeds

Put salt, sugar and oil in a large bowl. (Dissolve saffron in the hot water for additional flavor and color, if desired.) Add hot water and stir until sugar is dissolved. Cool to warm. Stir in yeast until dissolved. Add the eggs and mix in about 4½ cups flour to form a dough.

Cover board with ½ cup flour, knead dough on it until smooth and elastic, about 5 minutes, adding more flour if needed. Place in a greased bowl and turn dough to grease all over. Cover and let rise in warm place until double, about 1½ hours.

Punch down and divide into 4 equal parts. Roll each portion between hands to form ropes about 21" long. Place the 4 strips lengthwise on a lightly greased cookie sheet, pinch one end together and braid as follows: Pick up the rope on the right, bring it over the next one and under the third and over the fourth. Repeat, always starting on the right, until the braid is complete. Cut ends evenly, reserving about ½ cup dough; tuck ends under and pinch to seal. Roll reserved dough into a 15" rope. Divide into 3 parts and make a 3-stranded braid. Place small braid on top of larger braid. Cover lightly and let rise until double, about 1 hour.

Spread egg yolk mixture evenly over braids with brush or fingers. Sprinkle with seeds. Bake at 375 degrees for 35-40 minutes until golden brown. Serve warm or cool.

Yield 1 large loaf

Challah is the traditional bread of the Jewish Sabbath and most holidays and affectionately referred to as "a warm twist" due to the braided dough and the fact that it is great served fresh from the oven.

Middle Eastern
Pita

Pocket Bread

1 pkg. dry yeast
½ tsp. sugar
1¼ c. warm water (110-115 degrees)
3 c. flour
1 tsp. salt

Dissolve yeast and sugar in warm water for 5 minutes. Mix flour and salt together in large bowl. Add dissolved yeast and mix well until dough forms a ball and bowl sides are clean. (May use hands.) Cover with cloth and let rest for 10 minutes. Knead dough on board until smooth, about 5 minutes. Place in bowl, cover and let rise 30 minutes.

Punch down, divide into 12 pieces, cover and let rest 10 minutes. Roll out into 5" rounds and place on lightly floured cookie sheets. Cover and let rise 15 minutes on each side. Bake in 475 degree oven for 5-6 minutes, turning over halfway through baking. Place immediately in plastic bag to keep breads soft. Use within a day or freeze.

Split and serve with desired filling of meats, salads, Falafel, or cut Pita in wedges and use as a dipper for Humus (see index) and other dips and spreads.

Yield 1 dozen

Jewish
Bagels

1 c. milk, scalded
¼ c. butter or margarine
1½ T. sugar
½ tsp. salt
1 pkg. dry yeast
1 egg, separated
3 c. flour
2 T. water

Combine milk, butter, sugar and salt. Cool to lukewarm (105-115 degrees). Dissolve yeast in milk mixture, then add lightly beaten egg white and flour. Turn out onto floured board and knead until smooth. Place in greased bowl, cover and let rise until double. Punch down and divide dough into 20 pieces. Shape each piece into a ½" thick roll. Shape roll into a ring, pressing ends together firmly to seal. Cover and let rise until double. Drop rings into hot, not boiling, water for 30 seconds on each side. Place rings on greased cookie sheet. Whisk the egg yolk with 2 tablespoons water and brush over tops to glaze. Bake at 400 degrees 25-30 minutes or until golden brown. Slice and serve.

Yield 20 bagels

To toast or not to toast, but always with cream cheese and sometimes with lox.

French
Brioche

1 pkg. dry yeast
¼ c. warm water (105-115
   degrees)
½ c. soft butter or margarine
⅓ c. sugar
½ tsp. salt
3½ c. flour
½ c. milk
4 eggs
1 T. sugar

Soften yeast in warm water. Thoroughly cream butter, ⅓ cup sugar and salt. Add 1 cup of the flour and the milk to creamed mixture. Beat 3 eggs and 1 egg yolk together (reserve egg white). Add softened yeast and eggs to creamed mixture and beat well.

Add remaining flour and beat for 5-8 minutes by hand. Cover; let rise in warm place until double, about 2 hours. Stir down. Cover and refrigerate overnight.

Stir down; turn out onto floured surface. Set aside ¼ of the dough. Cut remaining dough into 6 pieces; form each into 4 balls. With floured hands, tuck under cut edges. Place in greased muffin pans. Cut reserved dough in 4 wedges; divide each into 6 pieces. Shape in 24 small balls.

Make indentation in each large ball. Brush holes with water; press small balls into indentations. Cover; let rise until double, about 30 minutes. Combine 1 lightly beaten egg white and 1 tablespoon sugar; brush tops. Bake at 375 degrees for 15 minutes.

Yield 2 dozen

Norwegian
Lefse

With Potatoes

5 c. potatoes (white russet),
   peeled
½ c. light cream
1 tsp. salt
¼ c. melted butter
2¾ c. flour

Cook potatoes until done; drain, put through ricer and cool completely. Mix cream, salt, and melted butter in bowl. Alternately add the potatoes and flour, mixing well with hands, adding more flour if mixture is too moist. Divide dough in half and make two long rolls. Place in refrigerator for (30) thirty minutes. The dough rolls better if kept chilled.

Preheat lefse or electric griddle to 410 degrees. Slice off 1″ or 2″ pieces of dough. Roll into thin rounds on floured board. Do not over-flour the rounds or handle too much when rolling or lefse will be tough. Bake until little brown spots appear on the surface; turn and bake other side. A lefse stick or turner is useful for lifting the lefse onto the griddle and for turning.

Baked rounds should be placed on a towel and covered to prevent drying. Store in tight containers in cool place or refrigerator.

Yield 16-8″ rounds

Norwegian
Lefse

With Instant Potatoes

1 lb. instant potatoes
6½ c. boiling water
¾ c. margarine (1½ sticks)
1 c. cream
1 T. sugar
1 T. salt
4 c. flour

Mix potatoes, boiling water, margarine, cream, sugar, and salt. Let stand until cold. Add flour. Divide dough into four sections, then divide each of these into eight pieces. Roll out one at a time, paper-thin, on a floured board. Bake on a lefse griddle until little brown spots appear on the surface; turn and bake other side. When done, they should be soft but spotted.

Yield 32 rounds

Traditionally lefse was eaten wrapped around a piece of meat or fish. Now it is more common to butter a pie-shaped wedge and sprinkle it with cinnamon sugar and eat it rolled or folded.

Norwegian
Lefse

Without Potatoes

1 c. rye flour
1 c. whole wheat flour
2 T. sugar
⅓ c. soft butter
2 c. milk

Combine flour and sugar; mix in butter with pastry blender or forks. Add milk and mix. Divide into fifteen walnut-size pieces, roll out into circles, and bake on hot lefse or electric griddle at 450 degrees. These are very fragile and dry out quickly; therefore, make them a smaller size and cover well.

Yield 15 rounds

You'll be surprised that the flavor is similar to the potato lefse.

Indian
Naan Bread

Asian Bread

1 lb. flour (about 4 c.)
1 tsp. baking powder
1½ tsp. salt
1 tsp. sugar
1 egg
1 T. plain yogurt
1½ c. water

Mix dry ingredients in a bowl. Make a "well" in the center. Add egg and yogurt and then water, a little at a time. Use as much as needed to form a firm dough. When the dough "cleans" the side of the bowl, it is ready. Knead the dough a little on a floured board until it is elastic. Pinch off pieces to make about 1½" balls. Place them on a buttered pan. Cover with a damp cloth and let rest for 30 to 60 minutes.

To cook, pat and roll the balls into thin circles, about 6" in diameter. (They should look like tortillas.) Place on cookie sheet and bake in 450 degree oven until puffed and slightly brown, about 8-10 minutes. Serve warm with butter or pate.

Yield 10 rounds

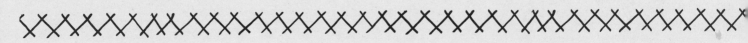

Eastern European
Grandma's Schnecken

Cinnamon Rolls

1 oz. cake yeast or 1 pkg. dry
  yeast
1 tsp. sugar
¼ c. warm water (105-115
  degrees)
½ c. flour
1 c. warm milk
¼ lb. soft butter
½ c. sugar
1 tsp. salt
6 eggs
½ pt. sour cream
6-7 c. flour
melted butter
½ c. sugar plus 1 tsp. cinnamon,
  mixed
1 c. melted butter
1 c. brown sugar
1 c. pecan halves

Make a sponge by dissolving yeast with 1 teaspoon sugar and warm water. Add ½ cup flour and milk; let stand. Cream butter and ½ cup sugar; add salt and eggs, one at a time, and then sour cream. When mixed, add sponge that has bubbled and enough flour to make a workable dough. Knead with hands until dough cleans side of bowl. Grease bowl and let dough rise covered in a warm place until double.

Punch down and let rise again; divide into quarters and knead each section until smooth. Roll out ½" thick into 6" x 12" rectangle. Brush generously with melted butter and sprinkle well with cinnamon-sugar mixture. Roll into a 12" long roll and slice crosswise about 1½" thick, to make 8 rolls. Put 1 tablespoon melted butter in each cup in large muffin tin and swirl it up sides with pastry brush. Place 1 generous tablespoon brown sugar and 3 pecan halves on top of butter; put in roll cut side down. Repeat with remaining dough, cover with cloth and let rise for 1 hour in a warm place. Bake in 350 degree oven for 25 minutes. Let cool slightly and turn out of pan while still warm.

Yield 32 large rolls

German
Stollen

Christmas Bread

3 pkg. dry yeast
½ c. lukewarm water (105-115
  degrees)
4 eggs
1 qt. milk, scalded and cooled
1¼ c. sugar
1 c. shortening
1½ T. salt
7 c. flour
¼ lb. mixed candied fruit
½ lb. raisins
½ c. chopped nuts
1 tsp. cardamom seed, crushed

Dissolve yeast in lukewarm water. Beat eggs, add cooled milk, sugar, shortening, salt and yeast mixture. Beat in ½ the flour. Add fruit, raisins, nuts and cardamom seed. Add enough flour to make dough easy to handle and not sticky. Knead until smooth. Let rise until double; shape into 4 or 5 round or oval loaves and let rise again.
Bake in 325 degree oven for 35 minutes on lightly greased cookie sheets. When cool, decorate with Powdered Sugar Frosting (see index) and red and green candied cherries. Bread can be braided, if desired.

Yield 4 or 5 loaves

Irish

Bannock

Irish Soda Bread

4 c. sifted flour
¼ c. sugar
1 tsp. salt
1 tsp. baking powder
¼ c. butter or margarine
2 c. seedless raisins
1⅓ c. buttermilk
1 egg
1 tsp. baking soda

Combine and sift flour, sugar, salt and baking powder. Cut in butter with pastry blender or 2 knives until it resembles coarse cornmeal. Stir in raisins. Combine buttermilk, egg and soda; add to flour mixture. Stir until just moistened. Bake in greased 1-quart pudding pan or casserole for 35-45 minutes in 375 degree oven or until golden brown.

Variations: Add caraway seeds to taste; substitute ½ cup molasses for ½ of the buttermilk and omit the sugar; use ½ whole wheat and ½ white flour.

Yield 1 loaf

Pieces should be broken off for serving instead of cut.

Swedish

Kafferbrod

Tea Ring

1 c. milk, scalded
¼ c. butter or margarine
½ c. sugar
1 tsp. salt
2 cakes yeast
¼ c. warm water (105-115 degrees)
2 eggs, well beaten
4½ c. flour
melted butter or margarine
brown sugar
cinnamon

Glaze:
1 c. powdered sugar
1 T. milk
½ tsp. vanilla

chopped nuts (optional)
candied cherries (optional)

Pour milk over butter, sugar and salt in large bowl. Cool to luke-warm. Crumble yeast into warm water in small bowl or measuring cup to soften. Add yeast to milk mixture. Add beaten eggs. Stir in flour to make a soft dough that is easy to handle.

Turn dough onto lightly floured surface and knead until smooth, about 5 minutes. Form into a ball and place in greased bowl; turn greased side up. Cover and let rise in warm place until double, about 1½ hours.

Divide dough in half. Shape one half into rectangle, 9" x 15" and ¼" thick, on lightly floured surface. Brush with melted butter and sprinkle with brown sugar and cinnamon. Roll in jelly-roll fashion, beginning at 15" side. Pinch edge of dough into roll to seal. With sealed edge down, shape into ring on lightly greased cookie sheet. Pinch ends together. With scissors, cut at 1" intervals almost through ring. Turn each section on its side. Repeat for second half of dough. Cover and let rise until double, about 30-45 minutes. Bake in 375 degree oven until golden brown, 20-30 minutes. Mix glaze ingredients until smooth and frost while warm. Decorate with chopped nuts and cherries, if desired.

Yield 2 ring-shaped loaves

Welsh
Bara Brith

Raisin Bread

1 pkg. yeast
¼ c. warm water (105-115 degrees)
2 c. milk, scalded
1 c. sugar
2 eggs
¼ c. melted butter
1 tsp. cinnamon
½ tsp. allspice
¼ tsp. cloves
6-6¼ c. flour
1 c. raisins

Dissolve yeast in warm water. Cool milk to lukewarm. Add sugar, eggs, butter and yeast mixture. Add spices and flour gradually until dough is no longer sticky. Add raisins and knead until smooth. Let rise until double. Punch down and let rise again. Form into 2 loaves, place in greased 8½" bread pans and let rise once more. Bake in 325 degree oven about 1 hour 15 minutes. Cool on racks.

Yield 2 loaves

Mexican
Sopaipillas

Fried Bread

4 c. sifted flour
1 tsp. baking powder
2 tsp. salt
¼ c. vegetable shortening
1⅓ c. cold water
honey for topping

Mix dry ingredients together in a bowl. Cut in shortening with a pastry blender. Add water, a little at a time, until dough holds together. Remove to floured board and knead slightly until smooth. Roll out with rolling pin until very thin. Cut into small squares or triangles, using a pastry cutter or knife. Heat 2" oil to 350 degrees in an electric fry pan, deep fryer, or heavy kettle. Fry sopaipillas until they puff up and turn golden. Turn over while frying. Drain on paper towels and serve warm topped with honey.

Yield 8 servings

American Indian
Indian Fried Bread

2 c. sifted flour
2 tsp. baking powder
½ tsp. salt
4 T. shortening (optional)
¾ c. milk
lard or vegetable shortening for deep frying
powdered sugar

Sift dry ingredients together. Cut in shortening, or if omitted, add milk directly to dry mixture. Cut in with knife until blended. Roll out on lightly floured surface. Cut in 3" wide strips, slash each in center. Fry in deep fat until brown, turn and fry on other side. Drain on paper towels. Shake in a sack of powdered sugar and serve hot.

Yield 16-20 pieces

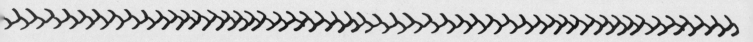

Spanish
Flour Tortillas

3 c. flour
2 tsp. salt
5 T. lard or shortening
¾ c. hot water

Mix flour and salt; cut in lard. Add hot water and knead. Pinch off in 1" pieces and knead to form patties. Roll out to 1/8" thickness. Cook on hot (375-400 degrees) ungreased griddle until spotted with a brown color. As each one cooks, stack together in a towel. These will hold heat for at least 30 minutes. As they get cold they will become brittle; reheat on a hot griddle and they soften. These are good stuffed with any cooked meat filling, shredded lettuce, sliced tomatoes, mushrooms, etc.

Yield 16 rounds

These can be deep fried after they have been cooked and stacked for a taco-like taste treat.

Icelandic
Flat Bread

¼-½ c. sugar
2 c. rye flour
2 c. white flour
3 tsp. baking powder
salt
boiling water

Combine dry ingredients and moisten with boiling water to dough consistency. Knead and roll out on floured board about ¼" thick. Cut circles around an 8" plate. Make a few cuts in each circle before baking. Bake on very hot cast-iron griddle and turn frequently. Spread with butter and serve with smoked lamb, pate, cheese, smoked herring, or whatever you desire.

Yield 10 rounds

Flat bread has been a favorite staple for all Scandinavians for centuries.

Swedish
Swedish Flat Bread

2 c. buttermilk
1¼ tsp. salt
½ c. sugar
½ c. melted butter
2 c. whole wheat flour
3¼ c. white flour
1 tsp. baking soda (scant)

Mix all ingredients together. Shape dough into 24 balls (about 2") and dip into flour. Roll into paper-thin rounds, prick with a fork all over top and bake on a cookie sheet in a 425 degree oven for 5-6 minutes or until edges start to turn brown. Bread should be crisp and tender. If it becomes tough, reheat before eating.

Yield 2 dozen 8" rounds

Norwegian
Telemarken Flatbröd

Flatbread

¼ c. lard
1 c. flour
1 c. white cornmeal
¼ tsp. salt
buttermilk, enough to moisten
    dough

Cut lard into dry ingredients with fork or fingers and add enough buttermilk to make dough of rolling consistency. Flour a board and take a piece of dough, about the size of a small egg, and roll out with flatbröd rolling pin until it is very thin. Lift up, using a flat stick or spatula, and place on an ungreased 400 degree lefse grill or electric griddle. Bake until lightly browned on both sides. Place on a rack in 325 degree oven until firmly set. Take out and stack. Store in a cool, dry place, wrapped in a towel. Serve with butter.

Yield 14 rounds

Wood coals and a takke iron were used in the old country. A grooved rolling pin was also used and is a prized possession in today's kitchens.

Mennonite
Zwieback

Dinner Buns

4 c. skim milk
2 pkg. dry yeast
½ c. sugar
1 c. vegetable oil
2 tsp. salt
6-7 c. flour (approximately)

Scald milk and cool to lukewarm (105-115 degrees). Dissolve yeast in milk. Add sugar. Then add oil and salt to dissolved yeast. Add enough flour to make a thin cake-like batter. Beat with electric mixer until soft. Add more flour to form a medium soft dough. Cover with cloth and let rise until double. Punch down, shape with floured hands into 1" balls for bottoms and ½" balls to be set on top of each bun. (The bottom part may need to be poked down in center before placing the top part on.) Place on greased cookie sheets, cover and let rise. Bake 15-20 minutes at 400 degrees. These freeze well.

Yield 6-7 dozen

Zwieback (pronounced with a "t" sound instead of a "z") is not the toast textured kind, but more like a bun.

Scottish
Tea Scones

2 c. flour
¼ tsp. salt
1 tsp. baking soda
2 tsp. cream of tartar
3 T. butter or margarine
½ c. milk

In large bowl, mix flour, salt, soda and cream of tartar. Cut in the butter with a pastry blender or rub it in with fingers until the flour-coated particles of butter are the size of coarse cornmeal. Add the milk all at once and mix to a soft consistency. Turn onto a floured board and knead very lightly until smooth. Roll to ½" thickness and cut out into rounds or triangles. Place on lightly greased cookie sheet; brush tops of scones with a little milk. Bake at 425 degrees for 10-12 minutes. Cool on wire rack.

Note: Scones can be baked on a griddle. Roll dough ¼" thick before cutting. Place on a moderately hot griddle (325 degrees) and bake 3-4 minutes until brown on the underside. Turn and bake 4-5 minutes more. Cool on a towel on a wire rack. Serve hot with butter and marmalade.

Yield about 2 dozen

Danish
Danish Kringle

A Sweet Yeast Bread

1 pkg. dry yeast
3 T. sugar
2 tsp. salt
1 c. lukewarm milk (105-115
    degrees)
3 egg yolks, beaten
4 c. sifted flour
½ c. shortening
½ c. butter
½ c. sugar
2 tsp. cinnamon
½ c. cream

Icing:
½ c. powdered sugar
1-2 T. cream
1½ T. melted butter
1/8 tsp. almond extract

Add yeast, sugar and salt to luke-warm milk. Stir until yeast is dissolved. Add the 3 beaten egg yolks. Sift flour into large bowl and cut in shortening and butter with a pastry blender. Add liquids to dry ingredients, mix thoroughly and put into greased bowl. Cover and store overnight in refrigerator.

Combine sugar and cinnamon. Cut dough into 4 equal parts. Roll each portion as thin as possible (1/16"). Place one piece of pastry on a lightly greased cookie sheet. Brush with cream. Sprinkle with cinnamon-sugar mixture. Top it with another layer of pastry. Brush with cream, sprinkle with cinnamon sugar. Place remaining pastry on second cookie sheet and repeat above procedure. Cover and let rise 2 hours. Bake at 325 degrees for 20-25 minutes. Mix icing ingredients and spread on warm rolls. Cut into 4" x 1½" rectangles. Can also use a prune filling between layers.

Yield 5 dozen pieces

Mmmmmmmmm — so good with coffee.

Jewish
Passover Popovers

½ c. butter or margarine
1½ c. water
1 tsp. sugar
½ tsp. salt
1½ c. matzo meal
6 eggs

In saucepan, boil together butter, water, sugar, and salt. Add matzo meal and mix thoroughly; let cool. Add eggs, one at a time, beating well after each addition. Bake in well-greased muffin tin or custard cups, ¾ full, for 45-55 minutes at 400 degrees. These are good hot or cold and can be filled to use as sandwiches.

Yield one dozen

A great bread replacement during the Passover holiday.

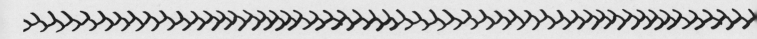

Yugoslavian
Potica

Rich Nut Roll

1 pkg. dry yeast
¼ c. warm water (105-115 degrees)
¾ c. milk
¼ c. butter or margarine
¼ c. sugar
1 egg
1 tsp. salt
3½-3¾ c. sifted flour

Walnut Filling:
½ c. honey
½ c. brown sugar, packed
¼ c. soft butter or margarine
1 egg, lightly beaten
2 T. milk
½ tsp. vanilla
2 c. finely ground walnuts

Dissolve yeast in warm water in large bowl. Heat milk and butter together until warm to touch. Add milk mixture, sugar, egg and salt to yeast. Stir well to blend. Add flour gradually, beating with wooden spoon, adding just enough to make a soft dough which leaves sides of bowl. Turn out onto floured board. Cover and let stand 10 minutes. Knead until smooth and elastic, about 5 minutes. Place dough in large greased bowl, turning to coat all sides. Cover bowl with plastic wrap, then a towel. Let rise in warm, draft-free place 1½-2 hours or until double. Punch down. Cover and let rest for 15 minutes.

Prepare filling by combining all ingredients, adding walnuts last. Place dough on large, lightly floured cloth. Roll dough out very thin into a rectangle about 20" x 30". Spread filling over dough, bringing to within 1" of edges. Starting at long side, roll up dough jelly-roll fashion by lifting cloth. Seal each turn by pinching edges into dough. Place on large greased cookie sheet, forming dough into snail shape. Tuck ends under. Let rise until light, 45-60 minutes. Bake at 325 degrees for 40-50 minutes. Cover with foil or brown paper if crust browns too quickly. Drizzle with powdered sugar glaze, if desired. Cool slightly before slicing.

This recipe makes one very large roll. To make 2 smaller rolls, dough may be divided in half and each half rolled out and filled according to directions.

Yield 1 large or 2 small rolls

You may need a large banquet table to roll out this dough!

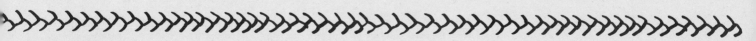

Bohemian
Kolacky

Filled Pastry Squares

½ c. sugar
1 pkg. dry yeast
2 c. warm milk (105-115 degrees)
6 c. flour (approximately)
½ c. melted vegetable shortening
2 tsp. salt
3 eggs, beaten

Fillings:
Prune:
1 lb. prunes
1 c. sugar
juice and grated rind of 1 lemon
¼ tsp. ground cloves

Cook prunes in water until tender; drain, pit and chop. Place in a pan and add sugar, lemon juice and rind and cloves. Cook over moderate heat 5 minutes.

Poppy Seed:
2 c. ground poppy seeds
½ c. white corn syrup
½ c. milk
½ c. sugar
1 T. butter
½ tsp. cinnamon

Place all ingredients in a pan and cook slowly over moderate heat 5 minutes.

Cheese:
1 lb. cottage cheese
2 egg yolks
pinch of salt
1½ c. sugar
½ tsp. grated lemon rind
2 T. melted butter

Combine cottage cheese, egg yolks, salt, sugar and lemon rind in a bowl. Mix well. Stir in butter.

To make the pastry squares, dissolve sugar and yeast in warm milk in a bowl. Add 2 cups flour and beat well. Add melted shortening, salt and beaten eggs. Add enough of remaining flour to make a soft dough. Place dough in greased bowl, cover and let rise until double.

Prepare filling of your choice.

To form kolackys, punch down dough. Divide in half and roll out on a floured board about ¼″ thick. Cut dough into 3″ squares, using a knife or pastry cutter. Place 1 teaspoonful of filling in each square and fold corners to center so they overlap. Use a little cold water on fingertip to help seal dough together. Place on a lightly greased pan, cover and let rise until nearly double. Bake at 350 degrees for 15-20 minutes or until nicely browned.

Yield 3 dozen

Norwegian
Julekake

Holiday Bread

2 pkg. dry yeast
½ c. warm water (105-115
  degrees)
1 c. milk, scalded
¼ c. butter
1 egg, beaten
½ c. sugar
2 tsp. salt
¾ tsp. freshly ground cardamom
½ c. candied cherries
½ c. diced citron
½ c. seedless raisins
5 c. flour (approximately)

Dissolve the yeast in warm water.
Place scalded milk, butter and egg
in a bowl. When lukewarm, add
the yeast. Add sugar, salt, cardamom and fruit to milk mixture.

Add 2 cups flour and beat in well.
Gradually add the remaining
flour, reserving some for knead-
ing. Knead on a floured board
until smooth. Place in a greased
bowl, cover and let rise until
double.

Punch down and divide dough
into two parts. Form round
loaves and place in greased pie
pans, cake pans or on cookie
sheets. Cover and let rise until
nearly double. Bake at 350
degrees for 30-40 minutes. While
warm, frost with Powdered Sugar
Frosting flavored with almond
(see index).

Yield 2 loaves

*When using cardamom, crushing or
grinding your own seeds removed
from the cardamom pods, gives a
better flavor than the already ground
cardamom.*

Norwegian
Quick Julekake

Candied Holiday Bread

½ c. soft butter
1 c. sugar
3 eggs
3 c. flour
3 tsp. baking powder
pinch of salt
1 tsp. freshly ground cardamom
½ c. lukewarm milk
½ c. water
½ c. raisins
1 c. mixed candied fruit (cherries
  and citron)

Cream butter and sugar; add
eggs, one at a time and mix well.
Combine flour, baking powder,
salt and cardamom; add alternately with milk and water to
butter mixture. Fold in raisins and
candied fruit. Shape into two
round or oblong loaves and place
on greased cookie sheet or in loaf
pans. Bake at 350 degrees for one
hour.

Yield 2 loaves

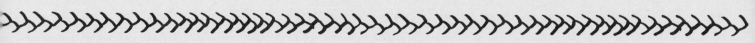

American
Doughnuts

2 eggs, beaten
1¼ c. sugar
1 tsp. salt
1 tsp. baking soda dissolved in
    1 c. buttermilk
1 tsp. nutmeg
1 tsp. vanilla
3½ c. flour
1 tsp. baking powder
3 T. melted shortening
2 lb. melted lard, for frying

Mix beaten eggs, sugar, salt and beat well. Add soda with buttermilk to this mixture. Add nutmeg, vanilla, and flour. Stir in baking powder and melted shortening, adding a little more flour if necessary to handle. Do not roll, but pat the dough out, cut with doughnut cutter and let stand for ten minutes. Deep-fry doughnuts in lard, turning until lightly brown and crisp. Drain on brown paper or paper towels.

Yield 2 dozen

American
Honey Jumbles

Doughnuts

3 eggs
1 c. sugar
1 tsp. salt
1½ c. honey
4½ c. flour
2 tsp. baking soda
1 tsp. ginger
1 tsp. vanilla

Beat eggs until thick and light colored. Continue to beat and add sugar and salt. Blend in honey, then mix with 1 cup flour, soda, ginger, and vanilla. Let stand overnight in refrigerator. In morning, add remaining flour, mix and chill. Roll out 3/8" thick. Cut with a doughnut cutter, then bake on a lightly greased cookie sheet in a 375 degree oven for 25-30 minutes.

Yield 2 dozen

American
Glazed Doughnuts

⅔ c. lard
4 T. sugar
1 T. salt
6 T. mashed potatoes
2 pkg. dry yeast
2¾ c. warm milk (105-115
    degrees)
2 eggs
8 c. flour
shortening for deep frying

Glaze:
⅓ c. boiling water
1 c. powdered sugar

Cream together lard, sugar, salt and mashed potatoes. Dissolve the yeast in warm milk; add yeast and eggs to potato mixture. Add flour and make a soft dough; it will be sticky. Let rise until double. Roll out dough and let rest a few minutes before cutting with doughnut cutter. Let rise again until double. Fry doughnuts and holes in deep fat at 360-375 degrees.
   Ice with glaze made by mixing boiling water and sugar together until smooth. Dip warm doughnuts and holes into warm glaze and cool on racks.

Yield 2½ dozen doughnuts, plus holes

heart of the meal

main courses

Scandinavian
Smørrebrød

Open-faced Sandwiches

Smørrebrød in Danish means buttered bread. An endless variety of sandwiches can be created using a thin half slice of well-buttered light or dark bread and adding a tasty topping and colorful garnish. Danish rye bread is recommended for most combinations, but white bread is preferable for mild cheeses, salmon, shrimp and pate. Garnishes include a wide range of colorful vegetables, such as sliced radishes, cucumbers, tomatoes, onions, beets, dill, parsley and pickles. Remoulade (see index), mayonnaise, mustard and flavored butter may be spread on the bread or piped on top. Smørrebrød should be eaten fresh with a knife and fork soon after they are prepared.

Traditional Smørrebrød combinations include:

- Thinly sliced rare roast beef with sliced gherkins and remoulade sauce.
- Sliced meat loaf with beet pickles and cucumbers.
- Beef tartare with capers, dill pickle and parsley.
- Sliced tomatoes and sliced hard-cooked eggs on lettuce leaf, piped with mayonnaise, garnished with chopped parsley.
- Fresh baby shrimp on lettuce leaf with mayonnaise and twists of lemon on top.
- Pickled herring on lettuce leaf with thin slices of Bermuda onion, slice of hard-cooked egg.
- Danish Tilsit or Swiss cheese with sliced radishes and mustard.
- Smoked salmon with egg (scrambled or sliced hard-cooked), chopped parsley or chives on top.
- Sliced roast beef with potato salad and chopped chives.
- Sliced ham with pickled cucumber and dark brown mustard.

Smørrebrød is nice for lunch, light supper or buffet snacks.

Icelandic

Baked Sole in White Wine

½ lb. fresh mushrooms
6 cold, cooked medium potatoes, thinly sliced
2 T. butter or margarine
1½ tsp. salt
½ tsp. white pepper
1 tsp. paprika
⅔ c. white wine
1 c. sour cream
2 lb. fresh fillets of sole or haddock, cut in serving pieces
parsley or chives, minced

Clean mushrooms, trim off tips of stems and slice. Arrange mushrooms on top of potatoes in a well-buttered ovenproof dish. Dot with butter and sprinkle with half of salt, pepper and paprika. Pour wine over potatoes and spread with half of the sour cream. Arrange pieces of fish over the top; sprinkle with remaining seasonings and cover with remaining sour cream. Bake 30-40 minutes in 325 degree oven or until fish flakes when tested with fork. Sprinkle with parsley.

6-8 servings

Greek

Psari Plaki

Baked Fish

1 c. finely chopped parsley
3-4 lb. halibut fillets or red snapper
salt and pepper
juice of 1 lemon
3 onions, thinly sliced
2 cloves garlic, minced
1 (8 oz.) can whole tomatoes
1 c. white wine
1 c. water
½ c. olive oil
2-3 fresh tomatoes, sliced
oregano

Grease a baking pan with olive oil and spread ½ cup chopped parsley on bottom of the pan. Lay the fish on the parsley, season with salt and pepper and drizzle lemon juice over the fish. Combine the remaining parsley, onions, garlic, canned tomatoes, wine, water and ½ cup olive oil; mix and pour over fish. Place fresh tomato slices on top and sprinkle with oregano. Bake at 350 degrees for 1 hour, basting occasionally. Nice served with cooked spinach, rice and Greek bread.

6 servings

Zorba would kick up his heels for this one!

American

Scalloped Oysters

½ lb. soda crackers, broken
2 cans whole oysters, save juice
2¾ c. milk
1½ T. butter

Place layer of crackers in 1½ quart well-buttered casserole. Alternate with layers of oysters and crackers. Dot last oyster layer with butter and end with layer of crackers. Mix oyster juice and milk and pour evenly over casserole. Bake at 350 degrees for 40 minutes or until browned.

3-4 servings

Japanese
Shrimp Tempura

Swedish
Stuvadefiskfileer

Creamed Fish

8 large raw shrimp
1 medium zucchini
1 medium carrot
1 medium onion
8 sprigs parsley
4 c. vegetable oil for frying
1 egg
1 c. cold water plus 2 ice cubes
1 tsp. baking soda
1 T. vegetable oil
1 c. flour

Dipping Sauce:
1 c. chicken broth
2 slices ginger root, peeled
1 T. dark soy sauce

Remove shells from shrimp, leaving tails on. Split shrimp along the back vein, cutting almost through the shrimp to make them lie flat; remove the veins. Rinse and pat dry.

Cut zucchini into 2" strips. Cut carrot into ¼" julienne strips. Cut onion into rings; separate parsley into sprigs. Pour 4 cups oil into wok and heat to 375 degrees. While oil heats, prepare tempura batter. In a small bowl, mix but do not beat, egg, water, ice cubes, soda and 1 tablespoon oil. Add flour; stir until just blended (batter will be lumpy).

Dip shrimp and vegetables individually into batter. Let excess batter drip off, then gently lower pieces into hot oil. Fry several pieces at a time without crowding; turn occasionally until crisp and lightly golden, about 2-3 minutes. Remove with slotted spoon, drain briefly and serve immediately.

As you fry, skim off and discard any bits of batter remaining in oil. To eat, dip each piece into tempura Dipping Sauce. To prepare the Sauce, in a saucepan combine ingredients and bring to a boil. Remove ginger slices and allow to cool.

4 servings
Yield 1 cup sauce

An oriental original tempered to fit your taste.

½ tsp. salt
½ tsp. white vinegar
1½ lb. fillets of cod or haddock
   (fresh or frozen, thawed)
2 T. butter
1 leek, sliced (or 2-3 green onions)
1 stalk celery, diced
1 carrot, sliced
2 tomatoes, sliced
pepper
1 T. flour
1 c. cream or milk

Mix salt and vinegar and rub into fillets. Heat 1 tablespoon butter and saute leek, celery and carrot. Do not brown. Layer fillets, tomatoes and vegetables in greased casserole. Sprinkle pepper between layers. Mix flour and cream until smooth and pour over fish. Dot with remaining butter. Cover and bake in 425 degree oven for 20-30 minutes.

4 servings

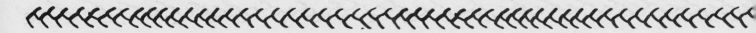

Coquilles St. Jacques au Cidre Doux

Scallops in White Wine

1 lb. sea scallops
7 T. butter
1 c. white wine
½ bay leaf
2 T. minced shallots
½ lb. fresh mushrooms, sliced
juice of ½ lemon
¼ c. flour
¾ c. heavy cream
½ tsp. salt
dash of freshly ground pepper

Saute scallops in 2 tablespoons butter a few seconds. Add wine, bay leaf and shallots. Add water, if needed, to cover. Bring to a boil, reduce heat and simmer covered 5-10 minutes. Remove scallops, reserving liquid.

In another pan, combine mushrooms, 2 tablespoons butter and lemon juice. Cover and simmer 10 minutes; drain and add this liquid to the wine broth and boil until reduced to about 1 cup. Remove bay leaf.

In a saucepan, melt 3 tablespoons butter; stir in flour. Remove from heat and slowly blend in the wine-mushroom liquid and the cream. Thicken slightly if necessary. Add the scallops and mushrooms; heat and stir until combined. Add salt and pepper to taste. Serve with rice pilaf or boiled potatoes.

4 servings

Voila!

Baked Lutefisk

2 lb. lutefisk
2 c. water
1 tsp. salt
melted butter

Rinse lutefisk well in cold water and soak overnight; drain. Place fish in glass or enamel pan (not aluminum). Add water and salt. Bake covered with foil at 400 degrees for 20 minutes or until done. Served with melted butter poured over the top. Accompany with boiled potatoes and lefse.

4-6 servings

Lutefisk is cod treated with lye which in the old days was prepared at home. Now we can buy it ready to cook, especially around Christmastime.

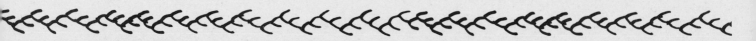

American Indian
Fried Fish

2 lb. small fillets of fish
1 tsp. salt
½ tsp. freshly ground pepper
¼ c. milk
½ c. flour
¼ c. yellow cornmeal
vegetable oil for frying

Pat fish very dry and dip into batter made from next five ingredients. Fry, turning, until golden brown.

3-4 servings

A great way to treat our Minnesota catch.

Chinese
Scallops with Pea Pods

1 lb. fresh or frozen scallops
½ tsp. cornstarch
¼ tsp. salt
1/8 tsp. sesame oil
½ tsp. light soy sauce
1/8 tsp. white pepper
1 T. cornstarch
2 T. oyster sauce or 1 T. dark soy sauce
¼ c. water
5 T. vegetable oil
4 slices fresh peeled ginger root, minced
1 clove garlic, minced
½ c. sliced bamboo shoots or water chestnuts
¼ c. chicken broth
½ lb. pea pods, strung and blanched
2 green onions, cut in 2" pieces

Rinse scallops well and pat dry. Cut in half, if large. Sprinkle ½ teaspoon cornstarch, salt, sesame oil, soy sauce and pepper over scallops. Mix well and allow to marinate for ½ hour. Combine 1 tablespoon cornstarch, oyster sauce and water in a small bowl, set aside.

Heat wok or large heavy skillet until hot. Add 3 tablespoons oil; when oil is very hot, add ginger, garlic and marinated scallops. Stir-fry until scallops are white, remove from wok and set aside. Wash, dry and reheat wok until hot. Add remaining 2 tablespoons oil, heat and add bamboo shoots, stir-fry 1 minute. Add chicken broth, bring to a boil, and add scallops. Add cornstarch mixture. (If gravy doesn't seem thick enough, add a little more cornstarch mixed with water.) Add pea pods, stir-fry until just heated through. Remove to hot serving platter, garnish with green onions, serve immediately with rice.

4-6 servings

An excellent easy company dish, beautiful to look at and delicious to eat.

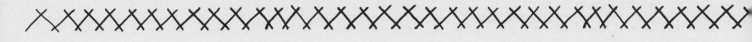

Welsh

Pasties

Meat and Potato Turnovers

6 c. sifted flour
3 tsp. salt
1½ tsp. baking powder
2 c. shortening or lard
1-1½ c. ice water
3 c. thinly sliced potatoes
1½ c. sliced carrots (optional)
1½ c. chopped rutabaga
  (optional)
3 c. chopped onion
salt and pepper
2 lb. beef sirloin, round or flank
  steak, cut in ½″ pieces
¾ lb. pork butt, ground or
  chopped (optional)
½ c. butter melted with ½ c.
  water

Mix flour, 3 teaspoons salt and baking powder in a large bowl. Add shortening and cut in with a pastry blender. Add ice water, a little at a time, until dough can be easily handled. Divide dough into 6 pieces, wrap in waxed paper and refrigerate for 30 minutes.

For each pasty: Roll out dough into a 9″ circle. Layer potatoes, carrots, rutabaga and onion; sprinkle with salt and pepper. Add beef, pork, more salt and pepper, ending with a second layer of potatoes. Fold in half, moistening edge with cold water, and seal edges. Crimp edge with a fork. Place on greased cookie sheet. In the top of each pasty, cut a small hole with a sharp knife.

Bake pasties in 425 degree preheated oven for 15 minutes. Turn oven to 350 degrees and bake 35-45 minutes or until they are nicely browned. After ½ hour of baking, remove from oven and spoon the butter-water mixture into the hole, return to oven and complete baking. Serve hot or cold. Pasties freeze and reheat well.

Yield 6 large pasties

Often referred to as Cornish Pasties and found in miners' lunchboxes.

Cuban

Cuban Stew

2 lb. beef chuck, cubed
¼ c. oil
1 T. salt
1 tsp. paprika
½ tsp. pepper
1 bay leaf
1 onion, sliced
3 cloves garlic, minced
1 green pepper, sliced
1 (8 oz.) can tomato sauce
1 c. dry sherry
1 c. water
2 lb. potatoes, peeled and cubed
1 c. small stuffed green olives

Saute beef in hot oil. Add salt, paprika, pepper, bay leaf, onion, garlic and green pepper. Cook a few minutes. Add tomato sauce, sherry and water and simmer covered 1½-2 hours or until meat is almost tender. Add potatoes and olives. Cook until potatoes are done, about 25-30 minutes. Add 1 cup more water or sherry when reheated.

6-8 servings

Try stewing over this one, you'll have no regrets.

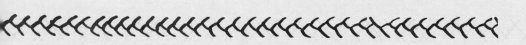

Chinese
Beef and Tomatoes

1 lb. beef flank steak, cut against
    grain into thin strips
2 tsp. light soy sauce
1 tsp. salt
pinch of pepper
6 T. vegetable oil
3 T. cornstarch
3 T. salted black beans
2 T. water
1 tsp. sugar
1 tsp. minced ginger root or ¼
    tsp. powdered ginger
1 tsp. minced garlic
1 small white onion, sliced
4 small firm unpeeled tomatoes,
    cut into eighths
½ c. chicken broth
2 green onions, cut into 2"
    lengths, including green tops

Marinate beef strips in mixture of
1 teaspoon soy sauce, salt, pepper
and 1 tablespoon oil for 30 minutes. Add 1 tablespoon cornstarch, mix well and set aside.
Soak black beans 10-15 minutes
in warm water, rinse, remove
skins and mash into paste. Mix
remaining 2 tablespoons cornstarch with remaining 1 teaspoon
soy sauce, water and sugar; set
aside.

Heat wok or heavy skillet until
hot. Add 3 tablespoons oil; when
oil is hot, add marinated beef and
ginger; stir-fry until both sides are
browned, about 2 minutes. Remove from wok. Set aside.

Wash, dry and reheat wok until
hot. Add remaining 2 tablespoons
oil, heat for 5 seconds. Add garlic, onion, bean paste and tomato
wedges. Stir-fry for ½ minute.
Add chicken broth and bring to a
boil. Stir in blended cornstarch
mixture and cook until sauce
thickens. Return beef and add
green onions to wok; stir for
another ½ minute or until beef is
reheated. Serve on heated platter
at once. May be accompanied by
boiled white rice.

4-6 servings

*This versatile dish can be made with
chicken or fish instead of beef.*

Korean
Bulgogi

Barbecued Beef

1 lb. beef sirloin or flank steak
2 T. sugar
¼ c. soy sauce
2 T. sesame oil
2 tsp. ground sesame seeds
¼ c. chopped green onions
⅔ tsp. garlic powder
⅔ tsp. black pepper

Slice beef against the grain into
¼" slices, 2"-3" long. Combine
the remaining ingredients, add
beef and marinate at room temperature 1-2 hours or overnight in
refrigerator. Place meat strips on
a rack over charcoal, on top shelf
of broiler or in electric fry pan.
Broil or grill until brown, 30-60
seconds on each side. Serve
immediately with hot rice and
stir-fry vegetables. Can also be
used as an appetizer.

4 servings

Chinese
Curry Beef

1 lb. beef sirloin or flank steak,
    cut against grain into thin slices
1 T. vegetable oil
1 tsp. light soy sauce
1 tsp. salt
1 T. cornstarch
4 T. vegetable oil
1 medium onion, cubed
1 tsp. minced garlic
1 T. curry powder
2 T. ketchup
2 green onions, cut into 2"
    lengths, including green tops

Marinate beef in mixture of 1 tablespoon vegetable oil, soy sauce and salt. Mix well and let stand for 30 minutes. Add cornstarch. Heat wok or large skillet, add 2 tablespoons oil and swirl up onto sides. Add marinated beef strips and stir-fry until almost browned, about 2 minutes. Remove beef and set aside. Wash and dry wok; then reheat. Pour 2 tablespoons oil into wok, add onion cubes and garlic; stir-fry until slightly brown. Add curry powder and ketchup; stir until well mixed. Return beef to wok, cook, stirring 1 minute, or until beef is reheated. Add green onions. Serve on heated platter, accompanied by rice.

4 servings

A spicy dish!

Japanese
Teriyaki Beef

2 T. vegetable oil
2 T. dark soy sauce
1 tsp. minced garlic
½ tsp. fresh minced ginger root
    or 1/8 tsp. powdered ginger
1 T. dry white wine
1 T. sugar
1½ lb. beef top round steak

Combine first six ingredients, pour over meat in glass dish and marinate 2 hours at room temperature or overnight in refrigerator. Remove from marinade and bake at 475 degrees for 12 minutes on each side if over 1" thick or 7-10 minutes each side if thinner. Serve in ¼" slices, hot or cold with stir-fry vegetables or lettuce salad.

4 servings

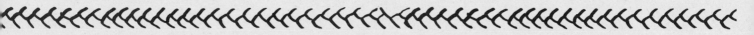

Hungarian
Gulyas

Beef Goulash

2-4 T. vegetable oil
2 lb. (8-10 medium) onions,
   chopped
2 lb. lean beef, cubed
1 clove garlic, crushed
1 tsp. marjoram
5 tsp. Hungarian paprika
salt and pepper to taste
3 c. boiling water
2 T. flour

In large skillet or Dutch oven, heat oil, add onions and saute until golden brown. Add beef and cook over medium heat, stirring, for about 30 minutes until beef loses its redness. Add garlic, cook a few minutes longer, then add marjoram, paprika, salt, pepper and 1 cup boiling water. Cover and simmer 30-45 minutes or until liquid is almost absorbed. Add second cup of boiling water, cover and simmer another 30-45 minutes. Add third cup of boiling water, cover and continue simmering until meat is tender, about 1 hour. Stir flour into pan juices to thicken. Season to taste. May be served over boiled noodles, potatoes or dumplings. Variations: *Faiker Gulyas:* After cooking for 2 hours, add 1½-2 cups uncooked peeled diced potatoes; continue cooking as directed above. Do not add flour to thicken gravy. Add ¼ teaspoon marjoram 15 minutes before serving. *Szegdyn-Gulyas:* Before serving, stir a 16 oz. can of sauerkraut (drained) into goulash, add a dash of caraway seed and heat thoroughly.

6-8 servings

A true Hungarian rhapsody!

Chinese
Moo Goo Ngow

Beef with Mushrooms

3 T. vegetable oil
1 clove garlic
1½ lb. beef round steak, cut in
  1/8" slices
salt and pepper
3 T. diced onion
1½ c. beef broth or bouillon
½ lb. fresh mushrooms, cleaned
  and sliced
1 T. soy sauce
3 T. cornstarch
water
4 c. hot cooked rice

Heat heavy skillet, add oil and garlic. Cook gently about 2 minutes; remove garlic. Add steak slices, salt, pepper and onion, cooking over moderate heat and stirring constantly until meat is browned. Add beef broth and mushrooms. Cover pan tightly and cook gently about 10 minutes or until meat is tender. Add soy sauce to cornstarch with enough water to make a thin paste. Mix well into broth, cooking over low heat and stirring constantly until broth thickens. Serve at once, with hot rice.

6 servings

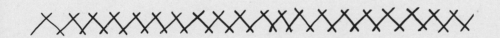

Jewish
Cholent

A Stewed or Baked Dish

3-4 lb. brisket of beef
3 medium onions, diced
3 T. oil
6 large potatoes, peeled and
    quartered
2 c. dried lima beans, soaked
    overnight
2 tsp. salt
¼ tsp. pepper
¼ tsp. paprika
½ tsp. seasoned salt
2 T. honey
¼ c. flour
boiling water

Brown meat and onions in oil in a
Dutch oven. Add potatoes,
beans, spices, honey and flour.
Cover with boiling water to 2"
above ingredients. Traditionally,
it is baked covered in a 400 degree
oven for 1 hour, then overnight at
225 degrees, but it may also be
baked in a 350 degree oven for 3-4
hours or simmered on top of the
stove 3-4 hours until meat is
tender.

6-8 servings

*Don't be "non-cholent" about the
energy crisis, consider using the
crockpot!*

German
Sauerbraten

3½-4 lb. beef chuck roast
2 onions, sliced
2 bay leaves
12 peppercorns
6 whole cloves
12 juniper berries (optional)
2 tsp. salt
1½ c. red wine vinegar
1 c. boiling water
2 T. shortening or oil
1 medium head cabbage, cut in 8
    wedges
12 gingersnaps, crushed
2 tsp. sugar

Wipe meat with damp cloth and
place in earthenware bowl, enamel or stainless steel pot. Combine
onions, bay leaves, peppercorns,
cloves, juniper berries, salt, vinegar and boiling water and pour
over meat. Cover and let stand in
refrigerator 3-6 days. Turn meat
twice a day with wooden spoons.
(Never pierce meat with a fork.)
    Remove meat from marinade.
Heat shortening in large heavy
skillet or Dutch oven; brown
meat slowly but well on all sides.
Add marinade; cover and simmer
2½-3 hours or until the meat is
thoroughly tender. Remove meat
and onions and keep warm.
Strain and measure liquid; add
water, if needed, to make 2½
cups. Pour liquid back into skillet; add cabbage wedges, cover
and simmer 10 minutes. Stir gingersnaps and sugar into liquid;
simmer 3 minutes more. Arrange
cabbage wedges on hot platter
with the meat and onions. Serve
gingersnap gravy alongside.
Sauerbraten is traditionally
accompanied by Spaetzle (see
index).

8-10 servings

*Ach, mein lieber, everyone loves
sauerbraten.*

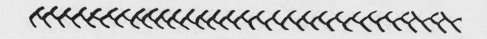

Chinese

Shredded Beef with Pepper

½ lb. beef, round, flank or sirloin
   steak
2 tsp. soy sauce
½ T. wine
1¼ c. peanut or vegetable oil
2 tsp. cornstarch
½ tsp. salt
3 green peppers
1 green onion
3 slices ginger root, peeled
1 tsp. salt
½ tsp. sugar

Shred (cut in small, thin pieces with large knife or cleaver) beef to 2" in length; mix well with soy sauce, wine, 1 tablespoon oil, cornstarch and ½ teaspoon salt and marinate for 1 hour. Clean green peppers, remove seeds, cut in halves and shred crosswise. Cut green onion into 1" lengths. Finely chop ginger root. Heat 1 cup oil in pan, stir-fry beef over high heat for about 20 seconds. Remove meat and drain. Heat another 3 tablespoons oil in pan. Stir-fry ginger root and green onion, then add beef, 1 teaspoon salt, sugar and stir well. Add green pepper, blend thoroughly and serve.

2-4 servings

French

Beef Bourguignon

¼ c. butter or margarine
1 T. vegetable oil
2½ lb. beef stew meat
1 medium onion, coarsely
   chopped
6 small green onions, chopped
4-6 carrots, sliced
2 T. flour
2 cloves garlic, mashed
1 (10 oz.) can beef bouillon plus
   ½ can water
1-2 T. tomato paste
1 bay leaf
pinch of thyme
1 tsp. salt
pepper to taste
2 or 3 sprigs parsley
1 T. Worcestershire sauce
2 c. Burgundy wine
1 lb. fresh mushrooms, sliced
3 T. butter

Melt ¼ cup butter and oil together in heavy skillet. Brown beef, onion and carrots slowly, 15-20 minutes. Sprinkle with flour to form crust. Add garlic, toss briefly. Add bouillon, water, tomato paste, seasonings, parsley, Worcestershire sauce and wine. Simmer covered over very low heat for 2 hours. (The liquid should barely bubble while cooking.) Saute mushrooms in 3 tablespoons butter; add to beef mixture and simmer covered another ½ hour.

6 servings

Try this with French bread for dipping in the sauce.

Greek
Souvlakia

Marinated Lamb Skewers

2 lb. boneless lean lamb
⅓ c. olive oil
3 T. lemon juice
1 large onion, chopped
1-2 cloves garlic, crushed
2 bay leaves, crumbled
2 tsp. oregano
1 tsp. salt
1 tsp. pepper
12 wooden skewers

Cut lamb into 1" cubes. Marinate meat in mixture made from remaining ingredients in glass dish for 2 hours. Divide meat evenly on 12 skewers that have been soaked in water for 1 hour to prevent burning. Grill the lamb about 4"-6" above the coals for 12 minutes, turning once. Serve with warm Pita Bread (see index).

6 servings

Shish kabob's kissin' cousin.

French Canadian
Tourtiere

Meat Pie

1 lb. lean ground pork
2 strips bacon, ground or finely diced
2 medium onions, finely chopped
1 clove garlic, minced
¾ c. water
1 tsp. salt
¼ tsp. pepper
¾ tsp. sage
¼ tsp. allspice
3 T. chopped fresh parsley
1 boiled potato, mashed

Crust:
2 c. flour
1¼ tsp. salt
½ c. butter
1 egg, beaten
¼ c. milk

Place pork, bacon, onions and garlic in a heavy skillet and cook, stirring for 5 minutes. Add next five ingredients, cover and cook 20 minutes. Remove from heat and stir in parsley and potato. Let cool.

Mix flour and 1¼ teaspoons salt in a bowl. Add butter and cut in with pastry blender. Mix egg and milk together and add to flour mixture. Form into 2 balls, wrap in waxed paper and refrigerate for 1 hour.

Roll out dough and line a 9" pie pan. Fill with meat mixture and top with second crust. Seal edges well. Make a few slits on top of pie and bake at 400 degrees for 45-60 minutes or until nicely browned. This can be frozen before baking.

6-8 servings

The tourtiere is traditionally served after midnight mass on Christmas, or at New Year's.

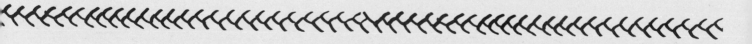

German
Rouladen

Beef Sirloin

8 pieces beef sirloin, round steak
　　or breakfast steak, thinly sliced
　　and pounded thinly
salt and pepper to taste
Dijon mustard
¼ c. minced onion
8 dill pickles, chopped (optional)
12 slices Canadian bacon,
　　chopped
flour for dredging
butter for browning
1½ c. beef broth
bay leaf
onion pierced with 2 or 3 cloves

Season beef slices with salt and
pepper. Spread with mustard.
Mix minced onion, pickles and
bacon. Place 1 tablespoon or
more of mixture on each piece of
steak, roll up and secure with 2 or
3 toothpicks. Dredge in flour,
brown in butter. Add broth, bay
leaf and onion and simmer covered over low heat 1¼ hours.
Serve with German Potato Pancakes (see index).

6-8 servings

French
Filet Aux Deux Poivres

Tenderloin with Peppercorns

1 T. green peppercorns, in natural
　　juice
2 T. cracked black peppercorns
salt to taste
4 (7 oz.) tenderloin or rib-eye
　　steaks
vegetable oil for sauteeing
½ c. cognac
½ c. port wine
1 c. cream
1 T. butter
1 T. Dijon mustard

Mix green and black peppercorns
and salt on plate and pat mixture
into both sides of steaks. Saute
steaks in hot oil to desired done-
ness; flame with warmed cognac,
remove steaks from pan and keep
hot. Add port wine and cook to
reduce sauce a little; add cream to
sauce and reduce some more.
Combine butter and mustard and
add to the sauce. Put steaks back
into warm sauce and serve.

4 servings

A seasoned popular party dish.

German
Jagerschnitzel

Hunter's Steak

2 lb. 1" thick beef steak or
　　venison, defatted and boned,
　　cut into bite-size pieces
salt, pepper and paprika
¼ c. butter or margarine
1 c. fresh sliced mushrooms or
　　chanterelle mushrooms
¼ c. chopped onion
⅔ c. red wine
1 c. sour cream

Sprinkle meat generously on both
sides with salt, pepper and paprika. Brown meat in butter for 5
minutes on each side. Remove
meat and add mushrooms and
onion to drippings. Saute 10-15
minutes, stirring occasionally and
adding butter if needed. Stir in
wine and sour cream, mixing
well. Bring to a slow simmer.
Add meat and let simmer 10 minutes more. Serve on egg noodles
or rice.

4-6 servings

English
Toad in the Hole

Steak Pie

1½ lb. beefsteak, cubed
½ tsp. salt
¼ tsp. pepper
2 eggs
1 c. flour
½ tsp. salt
2 c. milk

Cut beefsteak into cubes about 1″ square, leaving a few larger. Season with salt and pepper and place in a shallow, well-greased baking dish. Spread cubes apart so that batter can run between them.

Make a batter of remaining ingredients and pour over the beef cubes, making sure that some of the larger cubes have their "heads" sticking out of the batter. Bake in 425 degree oven for 30 minutes.

4 servings

Don't be discouraged by the Old English name. This is a very tasty dish!

American
Pounded Pepper Steak

4-1″ thick sirloin, club, filet mignon or round steaks, trimmed
2 tsp. salt
1 T. freshly crushed pepper
1 T. flour
shortening for frying

Place trimmed meat on waxed paper. Cover with half of the salt, pepper, flour and another piece of waxed paper, and pound it in, using the flat side of a meat cleaver, mallet or the edge of a sturdy plate. Repeat on opposite side. Cut meat into serving size pieces. Heat heavy skillet using enough shortening just to cover bottom. Place steak in pan and fry until crisp. about 3-5 minutes. Turn and cook to desired rareness. This is excellent served with sliced fresh tomatoes.

4 servings

Quick, easy and peppery.

Midwestern
Venison Steak

2 lb. venison, elk or moose
½ c. flour
1 T. dry mustard
1 tsp. sage
dash of salt and pepper
2 T. butter plus 2 T. oil for browning
1 c. red wine
1 large onion, diced
2 c. whole mushrooms
2 cloves garlic

Cut venison into thin steaks; wipe with damp cloth. Make seasoned flour with the dry mustard, sage, salt and pepper, and dredge steaks. Sear in butter and oil in heavy skillet. Pour red wine over the meat. Simmer covered on top of stove to thicken. Place in casserole and bake ½ hour at 325 degrees. Add onion, mushrooms and garlic and bake ½ hour longer at 325 degrees. Remove garlic before serving.

8 servings

For the hunters in the area.

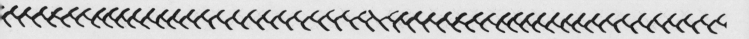

Irish
Lamb Stew

3½ lb. boned lamb shoulder or
   stew meat
1½ tsp. salt
¼ tsp. pepper
2 T. butter
2 medium onions, sliced
3 c. water
1 c. dry white wine
8 carrots, pared and quartered
4 large potatoes, pared and
   quartered
1 (10 oz.) package frozen peas
¼ c. flour
¼ c. chopped parsley

Trim fat from lamb and cut meat
into 2" cubes. Sprinkle with salt
and pepper. Heat butter in deep
saucepan, add onions and cook
until tender. Add lamb, 2½ cups
water and wine. Cover and simmer 1½ hours. Add carrots and
potatoes and cook 20 minutes.
Add peas and cook 15 minutes
more. Blend flour and remaining
½ cup water until smooth. Add
to stew and cook, stirring constantly until thickened. Place in
serving dish; garnish with
parsley.

6-8 servings

Stupendous for St. Patrick's Day!

East Indian
Lamb Curry

1 T. each coriander seeds, poppy
   seeds, salt
1 tsp. each red pepper, tumeric,
   powdered cumin, cardamom,
   ginger, nutmeg, mace, curry
   powder
12 whole cloves
15 peppercorns
fresh parsley or fresh coriander,
   chopped
¼ c. grated coconut
¼ c. ground almonds
2 large onions, chopped
6 large cloves garlic, minced
1 c. shortening or vegetable oil
4 medium tomatoes, quartered
1 pt. plain yogurt
6 lb. lamb, cubed
4 c. uncooked rice
pinch of saffron
¼ c. chopped cooked onion
¼ c. raisins
¼ c. cashew nuts

Mix spices, coconut and almonds
in flat pan. Place in 300 degree
oven for 5 minutes. Set aside.
Cook and stir onions and garlic in
shortening in Dutch oven over
medium-high heat until tender
and slightly browned, about 10
minutes. Stir in spices; add tomatoes, yogurt and meat. Simmer
loosely covered over medium-low
heat until meat is tender, about
1½ to 2 hours. Taste and adjust
seasonings. Cook rice according
to package directions, with the
pinch of saffron added. Garnish
rice with onion, raisins and
cashews.

8 servings

*Numerous regional variations of this
dish, some hotter than others, but all
a kind of Indian stew in which
poultry, meats, eggs, cheese or
vegetables are simmered with a long
list of spices.*

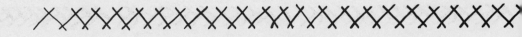

Mexican
Beef and Zucchini Skillet Dish

1 lb. ground beef
¼ tsp. dried red peppers or 4
    drops Tabasco
1 small onion, diced
½ tsp. cumin
1 clove garlic, crushed
pinch of basil
1 (8 oz.) can tomato sauce
1 lb. zucchini (3 medium), sliced
salt to taste

Brown ground beef, breaking up
with a fork; drain off fat. Add red
peppers, onion, cumin, garlic,
basil and tomato sauce. Simmer
10 minutes. Add zucchini, salt
and simmer again for 10 minutes.

4-6 servings

Lebanese
Baked Kibbeh

Pounded Lamb

1½ c. cracked wheat (bulgur)
2¾ lb. lean boneless lamb, finely
    ground
1 large onion, finely ground
2 tsp. salt
freshly ground pepper to taste
½ c. cold water
1 T. vegetable oil
¼ c. pine nuts
1/8 tsp. cinnamon
salt and pepper to taste
2 T. melted butter or margarine
    (optional)

In strainer rinse cracked wheat
thoroughly. Drain by squeezing
with hands. Combine cracked
wheat, ⅔ of the ground lamb,
onion, 2 teaspoons salt, pepper
and cold water in large bowl.
With hands, knead until mixture
is combined and smooth. Pat ½
of this mixture evenly into 10" x
15" jelly roll pan.

Brown remaining ⅓ of the
ground lamb in vegetable oil.
Add pine nuts, cinnamon and salt
and pepper. Spread mixture over
meat layer in pan. Cover filling
with remaining uncooked meat
mixture. Pat surface smooth.
Score top in diamond pattern
with knife. Bake at 350 degrees
for 25 minutes. If desired, drizzle
with melted butter and place
under broiler until browned.

To make meat easier to handle,
dip hands in cold water as necessary.

8-10 servings

*Often called the Lebanese national
dish, spelled Kibbi or Kibby, this can
be served cold as the near-eastern
version of steak tartar.*

Mexican

Bean and Beef Burritos

1 lb. ground beef
1 large potato with skin, diced
½ onion, chopped
1 T. vegetable oil
1 (4 oz.) can mild green chilies, diced
1 (15 oz.) can refried beans
salt, pepper and garlic salt to taste
12 flour tortillas
¾ c. shredded sharp Cheddar, Monterey Jack or longhorn cheese

Fry ground beef, potato and onion in oil, breaking up meat with fork. Drain off excess fat. Add green chilies and saute for 3 minutes. Add refried beans, salt, pepper and garlic salt. Place 2-3 heaping tablespoons of mixture in the center of each tortilla. Top with cheese. Roll up, tucking in edges. Place in 9" x 13" pan; cover with foil. Bake at 350 degrees for 20 minutes or fry individual burritos in hot oil until crisp. Can be done ahead and baked when needed.

Yield 12 burritos

Mexican

Beef and Bean Enchiladas ✻

1½ lb. ground beef
1 medium onion, chopped
1 (1 lb.) can refried beans
1 tsp. salt
1/8 tsp. garlic powder
⅓ c. canned or bottled taco sauce
1 c. quartered pitted ripe olives
2 (10 oz.) cans enchilada sauce
vegetable oil
12 corn tortillas
3 c. shredded Cheddar cheese (about 12 oz.)
sour cream

Saute ground beef and onion, breaking up with a fork until brown and crumbly. Stir in beans, salt, garlic powder, taco sauce and olives, reserving a few olives for garnish. Heat until bubbly. Heat enchilada sauce and pour half into ungreased, shallow 3-quart baking dish. Pour oil to a depth of about ¼" in skillet and heat. Dip tortillas, one at a time, in hot oil to soften; drain quickly. Place about ⅓ cup ground beef filling on each tortilla and roll to enclose filling. Place seam side down in sauce in baking dish. Pour remaining enchilada sauce evenly over tortillas; cover with cheese. Bake uncovered at 350 degrees for 25 minutes or until thoroughly heated. Garnish with pitted ripe olives and sour cream.

6 servings

A stay-at-home South of the border treat.

Scandinavian

Meat Loaf with Dill Pickle Sauce

1 lb. ground beef
½ lb. ground pork
1 medium onion, chopped
½ c. soft bread crumbs
½ c. dill pickle juice
1 egg
1 tsp. salt
½ tsp. pepper
¼ c. chopped dill pickles
½ c. ketchup
¼ c. water
2 tsp. sugar
1 tsp. Worcestershire sauce

Mix meat, onion, bread crumbs, pickle juice, egg, salt and pepper. Shape and put into medium-size loaf pan. Mix remaining ingredients and pour over loaf. Bake 1 hour and 15 minutes in 350 degree oven, basting often with juices from pan.

6 servings

Swedish

Kaldomar

Meat-Filled Cabbage Rolls

1 medium head cabbage
1 c. uncooked rice
2 medium onions, diced
¼ c. butter
1 c. bread crumbs
1 c. milk
2 eggs, beaten
2 lb. ground beef
1 T. sugar
2 T. salt
½ tsp. pepper
¼ tsp. nutmeg

Remove core and outer leaves from cabbage; cover with salted boiling water and boil for 5 minutes. Remove and drain cabbage. Add rice to this water and cook covered until tender. Drain the rice and reserve remaining liquid. Cook onions in 2 tablespoons butter until soft and yellow. Soak break crumbs in milk, then add rice, onions, eggs, meat, sugar, salt, pepper and nutmeg. Mold the mixture into rolls the size of an egg and place each on top of a cabbage leaf, wrapping the leaf around the meat. Secure with a toothpick. Place in deep casserole or roaster. Dot with remaining butter and pour on reserved liquid. Bake at 350 degrees for 1½ hours. Baste while baking. Delicious reheated. Also freezes well.

6-8 servings

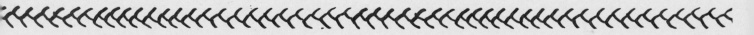

Swedish
Biff Lindstrom

Ground Beef Patties

1 lb. lean ground beef
2 eggs, beaten
1½ tsp. salt
pepper to taste
2 T. chopped onion
1 T. drained capers, finely
   chopped
¼ c. heavy cream
½ c. drained, finely chopped
   beets, fresh-cooked or canned
2 T. butter
2 T. vegetable oil

Mix together in a bowl, beef, eggs, seasonings, onion, capers and cream. Add the beets, mixing lightly. Shape into patties ¾" thick and about 2" in diameter. Heat the butter and oil in a skillet and fry patties over moderate heat until they are browned, about 5 minutes on each side. Remove patties and add a little water to the pan to thin out the juices. Pour this over the meat. Serve with fried egg on top of each patty, if desired.

4-6 servings

Fast-food shops and drive-ins can't compete with these hamburgers.

Greek
Moussaka

Eggplant Casserole

3 medium eggplant, unpeeled
salt
1½ lb. ground beef
6 medium onions, finely chopped
1 c. butter
2 tsp. chopped parsley
1 (28 oz.) can tomatoes
¼ c. red wine
salt and pepper
2 eggs, well beaten
¾ c. grated cheese (Kefaloteril or
   Romano)
6 T. bread crumbs

Cream Sauce:
6 T. butter
7 T. flour
1 tsp. salt
dash of nutmeg
3 c. milk

Slice and salt eggplant; let stand. Brown beef and onions in ½ cup butter. Add parsley, tomatoes, wine, salt and pepper. Simmer until liquid is absorbed; set aside until cool. Add eggs, ½ cup cheese and 3 tablespoons bread crumbs. Mix well. Fry each slice of eggplant in remaining butter, browning both sides. Set aside. In 9" x 13" pan, sprinkle remaining bread crumbs. Arrange layers of eggplant slices alternately with meat mixture, ending with eggplant.

To make cream sauce, use a heavy saucepan and melt butter; blend in flour, salt and nutmeg. Slowly add milk, stirring constantly. Continue to cook and stir until thickened. Top eggplant slices with cream sauce, sprinkle with remaining ¼ cup grated cheese. Bake in 375-400 degree oven for 1 hour.

8-10 servings

Magnificent Moussaka made for festive occasions. A Greek specialty.

Swedish
Swedish Meatballs

1 c. bread crumbs
1 c. milk
1 egg, beaten
½ tsp. salt
¼ tsp. pepper
½ tsp. allspice
½ tsp. nutmeg
½ lb. ground pork
1 lb. ground round steak
1 medium onion, minced
4 T. vegetable shortening
2 T. flour
2 c. light cream or water

Soak bread crumbs in milk. Add egg, salt, pepper, allspice and nutmeg and mix thoroughly with the ground meat. Add onion. Shape into small balls and brown on all sides in hot shortening. Make gravy by adding flour and cream. Cover frying pan and simmer meatballs in gravy for 1 hour.

Yield 3 dozen

Every family has a favorite meatball.

German
Sauerbraten Beef Balls

1 lb. lean ground beef
1 tsp. salt
½ c. chopped onion
dash of pepper
⅔ c. evaporated milk
2 T. shortening
Sauce:
2 T. vinegar
2 T. ketchup
1 T. brown sugar
8 peppercorns, crushed
½ tsp. salt
⅓ c. raisins
¼ c. bread crumbs
6 gingersnaps, crushed
1 bay leaf
½ cup water

Mix first five ingredients and roll into small balls. Fry in hot shortening and place in a casserole. Mix sauce ingredients and heat. Pour over meatballs and bake tightly covered in a 350 degree oven for 30 minutes.

6-8 servings

Danish
Frikadeller

Meatballs

½ lb. veal
½ lb. pork
1 onion, grated
3 T. flour
1¼ c. club soda or milk
1 egg, beaten
1 tsp. salt
¼ tsp. pepper
1/8 tsp. allspice
3 T. butter or margarine
3 T. salad oil

Grind the veal and pork together several times and place in a large mixing bowl. Add onion; mix well. Beat flour into meat mixture, gradually adding the club soda, continuing to beat until mixture is fluffy. Beat in egg, salt, pepper and allspice. Cover the bowl and refrigerate for 1 hour.

Shape into oval patties or balls. Melt butter and oil in a large skillet. Brown meatballs a few at a time until thoroughly cooked. (Because of the pork content, never serve these rare.) When brown and cooked, remove and keep warm until served. Serve accompanied by boiled potatoes and pickled beets.

4-6 servings

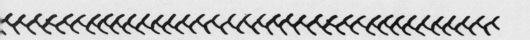

Italian
"South Americans"

1 pepperoni sausage (about 5")
2 large green peppers
3 medium onions
1 stalk celery
2 green chili peppers (from 4 oz. can)
3 lb. ground beef
1 (8 oz.) can mushroom stems and pieces
1 (6 oz.) can tomato paste
⅓ c. water
¼-½ tsp. pepper
1½-2 tsp. salt
Tabasco sauce to taste

Coarsely grind pepperoni, green peppers, onions, celery and chili peppers. (May be chopped fine in food grinder.) In large skillet, brown ground beef, drain off fat and add ground pepperoni-vegetable mixture. Cook until just tender, stirring frequently. Add mushrooms (do not drain), tomato paste, water and seasonings. Cover and simmer over low heat 30-45 minutes.

Serve mixture spooned over split hard rolls or thick slices of Italian or French bread.

This mixture freezes well.

8 servings

These Italian South Americans add a real spice to life.

Jewish
Prakes

Stuffed Cabbage

3 onions, diced
1 T. chicken fat or butter
¼ tsp. pepper
1 c. water
3 T. sugar
1 (20 oz.) can tomatoes
juice of 1 lemon (2 T.)
1 tsp. salt
1 large head cabbage
1½ lb. ground beef
2 eggs
1 tsp. salt
1/8 tsp. pepper

Brown onions in Dutch oven in the chicken fat. Add ¼ teaspoon pepper, water and sugar. Mix tomatoes, lemon juice and 1 teaspoon salt; simmer for 30 minutes.

Remove core and place cabbage in boiling water; remove from heat and let stand 20 minutes. Pull leaves apart gently and trim thick center vein. Combine beef, eggs, 1 teaspoon salt and 1/8 teaspoon pepper. Place 1 tablespoon meat mixture on each cabbage leaf and roll up by bringing opposite sides together over meat. Overlap and roll. Place in heated sauce, seam side down, cover and simmer 1 hour. Can stretch recipe by adding 1½ cups cooked rice to meat.

6-8 servings

Croatian
Sarma

Stuffed Cabbage Leaves

½ lb. ground pork
½ lb. ground beef
1½ tsp. salt
¼ tsp. pepper
½ c. uncooked rice
1 small onion
1 medium potato, peeled
1 clove garlic
2 eggs
10-12 large cabbage leaves
1 (20 oz.) can sauerkraut (or 2 cups fresh)

Combine pork and beef with salt, pepper and rice. Grind onion, potato and garlic in a meat grinder or food processor. Combine with meat mixture; add eggs and mix very well. Remove core and outer leaves from head of cabbage. Submerge cabbage in boiling water. Continue boiling, carefully removing leaves of cabbage as they loosen. When leaves are cool, trim thick center vein, place some of meat mixture near core end and roll up, tucking in ends. Layer the rolls with sauerkraut in a heavy casserole. Cover and bake at 350 degrees for 1½ hours. Check while baking and add a small amount of water, if needed.

6-8 servings

Italian
Pizza Rustica Toscano

Holiday Main Dish Pie

pastry for two 12" pies
2 lb. fresh Ricotta cheese
1 lb. fresh Mozzarella cheese, diced
4 oz. Parmesan or Romano cheese, grated
4 eggs
¼ c. fresh minced parsley
¼ c. diced Genoa salami or pepperoni
¼ lb. ham or cooked Italian sausage, diced
salt
freshly ground pepper
nutmeg

Roll out pastry and cover both pie pans with bottom crust. Mix cheeses, eggs, parsley, meats, salt and pepper together thoroughly. Divide mixture between crusts. Sprinkle nutmeg on top. Bake at 300 degrees for 1 hour or until tops are golden. Serve warm or cold. This is especially good reheated.

Yield 2 pies

Italian Quiche . . .

Minnesota
Roast Turkey

¼ lb. melted butter
3 cloves garlic, mashed
¼ tsp. ginger
½ tsp. seasoned salt
1/8 tsp. paprika
flour
10 lb. turkey

Combine the first six ingredients, using enough flour to make paste. With hands, rub mixture inside and outside of turkey. Place in large pan and bake uncovered at 325 degrees for 2½ hours or until brown, basting often. Cover with aluminum foil tent and cook for 2½ hours or more until turkey is done and leg moves easily. May stuff with your favorite dressing.

8-10 servings

A seasoned Thanksgiving tradition, can be done with roast chicken also and served all year long.

German
Pork Hocks and Sauerkraut

2 pork hocks
water to cover
½ tsp. salt
1/8 tsp. pepper
1 medium onion, quartered
2 stalks celery, sliced
3½ c. sauerkraut
brown sugar

Boil hocks in water with salt, pepper, onion and celery. Cook until tender, about 3 hours. Remove meat and cool. Trim lean meat off hocks and skim fat off broth. (Can be put in freezer a few minutes to solidify fat for easy removal.) Put broth and sauerkraut in a roaster. Lightly sprinkle with brown sugar. Add meat and cover. Bake at 350 degrees for about 2 hours. Serve with boiled buttered potatoes.

4-6 servings

Danish
Stuffed Pork Loin

3-4 lb. boned pork loin
2 tsp. salt
½ tsp. pepper
1 tsp. ginger
12 pitted prunes
¾ c. boiling water
1 tart apple
1 tsp. lemon juice
3 T. butter
3 T. vegetable oil
1-2 T. flour
¾ c. dry white wine
¾ c. light cream
1 T. red currant jelly

Make a hole straight through the center of the loin. Season meat with salt, pepper and ginger. Cover prunes with boiling water and soak 30 minutes; drain. Peel and slice apple and sprinkle with lemon juice. Mix prunes and apple together and stuff mixture into center of loin with a larding needle or handle of a wooden spoon. Tie string around loin at 1" intervals. Brown meat on all sides in butter and oil. Roast in 325 degree oven for approximately 2 hours or until pork is no longer pink. Remove loin, add flour to drippings and whisk in the wine and cream. Stir in currant jelly and mix well. Slice meat and serve with sauce.

4-6 servings

Polish
Pork Chops in Wine Sauce

4-1" thick pork chops
2 T. butter
½ c. finely chopped onion
½ lb. sliced fresh mushrooms
1 c. dry white wine
1 tsp. dill weed

Brown chops on both sides in butter; remove from skillet. Add onion and mushrooms, lightly saute. Return chops to skillet; add wine, cover and simmer 1 hour or until fork tender. Sprinkle with dill weed.

4 servings

Japanese
Ginger Pork

1 piece fresh ginger root, 2" long
3 T. soy sauce
1 T. sugar
1 tsp. sake or dry sherry
pinch of salt
1-1½ lb. thinly sliced lean pork chops
1 T. vegetable oil

Peel ginger and grate to make 1 teaspoon. Slice remaining ginger into pieces. Set aside. Mix grated ginger with soy sauce, sugar, sake and salt. Marinate pork chops in mixture for 10 minutes. Heat skillet over medium heat; add oil; fry marinated pork and ginger slices on both sides until brown. Add any leftover marinade sauce and cover. Cook several minutes over low heat until pork is tender. Serve with rice and a stir-fry vegetable.

4 servings

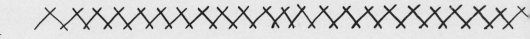

Chinese

Shredded Pork with Cabbage

1 lb. lean pork, shredded in very thin strips
1 tsp. salt
½ tsp. pepper
½ tsp. sugar
2 T. cornstarch
1 tsp. light soy sauce
6 dried black mushrooms
2 tsp. water
1 T. dark soy sauce
¼ c. vegetable oil
1 tsp. minced ginger root or ¼ tsp. powdered ginger
2 c. shredded cabbage (bok choy or celery cabbage if available)
4 oz. canned bamboo shoots, shredded in very thin strips
½ c. chicken broth
2 green onions, cut in 2" lengths, including green tops

Marinate pork strips in salt, pepper, sugar, 1 tablespoon cornstarch and light soy sauce for ½ hour. Soak black mushrooms in warm water to cover until soft, 10-15 minutes. Wash, pat dry, discard stems, cut in thin strips and set aside. Mix remaining 1 tablespoon cornstarch with 2 teaspoons water and dark soy sauce. Set aside.

Heat wok or heavy skillet until very hot. Add oil; heat for 2 minutes; add ginger and pork and stir-fry until all pork strips turn white, 2-3 minutes. Add black mushrooms, cabbage and bamboo shoots; stir-fry 1 minute. Add chicken broth and cook to boiling. Stir in blended cornstarch mixture and cook until sauce thickens. Add green onions and stir-fry ½ minute. Remove from wok to heated platter and serve at once with rice. Can add shredded carrots or red pepper for more color.

4 servings

Chinese

Chicken with Black Mushrooms

10 dried black mushrooms
3 lb. chicken, boned
½ lb. lean pork steak
1 T. peanut oil
½ tsp. chopped fresh ginger root
1 tsp. salt
2 T. rice wine
1 tsp. cornstarch
½ c. water
½ c. sliced water chestnuts
3 green onions, chopped
parsley

Soak mushrooms in warm water until soft, about 15 minutes. Drain and cut in small pieces. Cut chicken and pork into small bite-sized pieces and brown in oil. Combine remaining ingredients except onions and parsley. Add meat and mushrooms. Pour into baking dish and bake covered in 375 degree oven for 20 minutes; then at 350 degrees for 40 minutes. Stir once or twice during baking. Garnish with green onions and parsley. Serve with rice.

4-6 servings

Lebanese

Djaj Ma'a Limoon

Marinated Chicken

2 cloves garlic, mashed
1 tsp. salt
dash of pepper
1 c. vegetable oil
½ c. lemon juice
2 cut-up chicken fryers

Combine mashed garlic, salt, pepper, vegetable oil and lemon juice. Stir well. Marinate chicken pieces in this dressing for 1 hour. Drain and save marinade. Place chicken in open roaster, bake at 350 degrees approximately 1 hour or until tender, basting occasionally with remaining marinade.

6-8 servings

Lebanese

Djaj Mehshe

Stuffed Roasted Chicken

4-6 lb. chicken or capon
1 gizzard, minced
1 medium onion, minced
3 T. butter
3 T. pine nuts, browned in butter
1 tsp. salt
1/8 tsp. allspice
1/8 tsp. cloves
1/8 tsp. cinnamon
pepper to taste
1 c. rice, partially cooked (10 min.)

Clean chicken and soak ½ hour in salt water; drain and dry. Saute gizzard and onion in butter. Add browned pine nuts, seasonings and partially cooked rice. Stuff chicken with rice mixture. Sew the opening or close with small skewers. Roast in open pan in 300 degree oven about 40 minutes per pound. During last half hour baste chicken with drippings.

Extra stuffing may be baked in separate casserole, adding drippings from the chicken.

4-6 servings

Yugoslavian

Rezot

Chicken with Rice

1 medium onion, chopped
vegetable oil for browning
1 chicken fryer, cut up
1½ c. uncooked rice
1 carrot, grated
2 tsp. minced parsley
salt and pepper to taste
½ bay leaf (optional)
½ tsp. thyme (optional)
2¼ c. water

Saute onion in hot oil until soft; add chicken pieces and fry until brown. Lower heat, cover and cook about 20 minutes. Add rice, carrot, parsley, seasonings and water. Cover and continue cooking until rice is done, about 30-40 minutes, adding water as necessary.

4-6 servings

For a special treat use veal instead of chicken.

Yugoslavian
Mushki

Eggplant Dish

2 medium eggplant, unpeeled,
  sliced ¼" thick
1½ tsp. salt
1 large onion, sliced
1 T. butter
1-2 cloves garlic, mashed
½ tsp. thyme
1½ T. chopped parsley
1½ tsp. black pepper
flour
oil for frying
½ lb. Swiss cheese, sliced
½ lb. smoked ham, thinly sliced
⅓ c. grated Parmesan cheese
2 tsp. paprika
¼ tsp. nutmeg
3 eggs with cream to equal 1⅓ c.

Sprinkle eggplant with 1 teaspoon salt and let stand ½ hour. Saute onion slices in butter with garlic, thyme, parsley and 1 teaspoon pepper until onion becomes transparent. Drain excess water from eggplant and dry with paper towels, then dredge eggplant in flour and deep fry in oil.

Place a layer of eggplant in a buttered 7" x 12" pan and cover with onion, then cheese and ham. Repeat layering twice. Sprinkle with Parmesan cheese and paprika. Add ½ teaspoon salt, ½ teaspoon pepper and nutmeg to egg mixture and pour over casserole. Bake in a 325 degree oven for 1 hour.

8 servings

French
Chicken Cassoulet

½ lb. sweet Italian link sausage
1 medium onion, diced
2 T. vegetable oil
3½-4 lb. chicken fryer, cut up
½ tsp. salt
¼ tsp. pepper
1 (14½ oz.) can tomatoes
1 medium green pepper
1 (15 oz.) can white or red kidney
  beans
¼ tsp. hot pepper sauce
1 tsp. Worcestershire sauce

Cut sausage into chunks. Cook onion and sausage in hot oil until sausage is brown. Push to one side and brown chicken pieces in same skillet. Remove chicken; add salt, pepper, tomatoes and green pepper. Pour this mixture into casserole and add beans, hot pepper sauce and Worcestershire sauce. Mix well. Add chicken and cover. Bake in 350 degree oven for 45 minutes or until chicken is tender.

4 servings

A full meal for families of four.

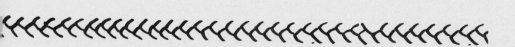

Chicken Verde

Chicken Pablano

Chicken Adobo

½ c. fresh coriander (cilantro), loosely packed
2 c. chopped onion
1 clove garlic, minced
1 (10 oz.) can tomatillos (green tomatoes)
½ (4 oz.) can chopped green chili peppers, drained
salt and pepper
2½ lb. chicken fryer, cut up
3 T. lard or shortening

Combine coriander, onion, garlic, tomatillos, green chili peppers and salt and pepper to taste in blender. In heavy skillet, brown chicken pieces lightly in hot lard. Pour sauce mixture over browned chicken, cover and simmer on top of stove for 1¼ hours.

4 servings

3 whole chicken breasts, cut in halves
½ c. olive oil
2 large onions, sliced
2 cloves garlic, minced
salt and pepper
1 (4 oz.) can mild green chilies, diced
1 pt. sour cream

Simmer chicken in olive oil about 30 minutes or until tender. Cool and pull meat from bones in long pieces. Discard skin and bones. Add onions and minced garlic to remaining oil in skillet. Add salt and pepper to taste and diced chilies. Cook until onions are transparent. Return chicken to mixture in pan and add sour cream. Heat thoroughly but do not allow to boil. Serve with warm buttered tortillas.

6 servings

Even with mild chilies, this is a very hot dish.

2½-3 lb. chicken fryer, cut in serving pieces
½ c. vinegar
4 tsp. soy sauce
1 clove garlic, minced
1 tsp. freshly ground pepper
2 c. water
½ bay leaf
4 c. cooked rice

Arrange chicken pieces in a large heavy skillet. Combine remaining ingredients except rice and pour over chicken. Bring to boiling; reduce heat to simmer. Cover and continue to simmer until chicken is tender, about 1 hour. Remove cover, increase heat to medium and cook until all liquid evaporates and chicken begins to fry. Turn as necessary and fry until the chicken is browned on all sides. Serve with the hot cooked rice.

4 servings

German
Stewed Chicken

1 stewing hen (or large fryer), cut
  in serving pieces
salt, pepper, garlic powder and
  paprika
3 stalks celery, cut in 1"-1½"
  pieces
3 large carrots, cut in 1"-1½"
  pieces
1 medium onion, chunked
1 c. canned tomatoes or 2 small
  ripe tomatoes, peeled and
  quartered
salt and pepper
1 T. water

Layer chicken pieces in a heavy
casserole or Dutch oven, placing
heavier pieces on the bottom and
season each layer well with salt,
pepper, garlic powder and paprika. Place vegetables on top and
sprinkle with salt and pepper.
Add 1 tablespoon water, cover
tightly and simmer 3-4 hours or
until tender.

6-8 servings

*Could this be where they got the
slogan "A chicken in every pot"?*

Cuban
Chicken Rice
Casserole

3 cloves garlic, minced
¾ c. grapefruit juice
2 (2½ lb.) chicken fryers, cut up
1 (4 oz.) jar pimentos, mashed
1 (17 oz.) can peas or 1 (10 oz.)
  pkg. frozen peas
1 (15 oz.) can asparagus spears
  (optional)
1 (12 oz.) can beer
⅓ c. vegetable oil
1 large green pepper, seeded and
  chopped
1 large onion, minced
1 (16 oz.) can tomato sauce
2 T. salt
½ tsp. freshly ground pepper
1 bay leaf
2 chicken bouillon cubes
4 c. uncooked long grain rice
pinch of saffron (optional)

Combine garlic and grapefruit
juice; pour over chicken pieces in
a shallow glass pan. Marinate 2-4
hours in the refrigerator, basting
occasionally. Remove chicken
from marinade. Drain liquid from
pimentos, peas and asparagus;
add to chicken marinade and
beer. Add enough water to measure 8 cups. Set aside.

  In a large Dutch oven, heat oil
and brown chicken, a few pieces
at a time. Return all the chicken
to the Dutch oven, add the green
pepper, onion, tomato sauce and
the 8 cups of liquid. Cover and
cook over low heat about 30 minutes. Stir in salt, pepper, bay leaf,
bouillon cubes, rice and saffron;
cover and cook about 20 minutes
or until rice is tender. Add more
liquid if necessary. Add peas,
asparagus and pimentos and heat
thoroughly. This casserole may
be prepared in advance and
frozen.

10-12 servings

Polish

Chicken Polanaise

Chicken Patties with Dill Sauce

½ c. butter
1½ c. chicken broth
4 slices white bread
3 lb. ground chicken
3 eggs
1 T. Maggi liquid seasoning
4 T. chopped fresh dill or 2 T. dry
   dill weed
salt and pepper
¼ c. flour
1 T. butter
1 T. vegetable oil
½ pt. whipping cream

Melt ½ cup butter and add the chicken broth. Soak bread in this mixture. Combine chicken, bread mixture, eggs, Maggi liquid and ½ of the dill. Mix well. Refrigerate for ½ hour. Season to taste with salt and pepper. Form patties about 1½"-2" in diameter. Roll in flour and fry in 1 tablespoon butter and oil until golden, but not brown, on both sides. Arrange patties in baking dish. Cover with cream and sprinkle on remaining dill. Bake covered at 325 degrees for 20 minutes. Uncover and bake ½ hour longer. Serve with rice.

6-8 servings

What came first — this chicken or Chopin's Polanaise?

Hungarian

Partridge Pie

6 strips bacon
3 partridge, grouse or quail
3 c. sherry
3 potatoes, diced
1 onion, diced
2 carrots, diced
1 tsp. salt
½ tsp. pepper
1/8 tsp. sage
1 clove garlic, minced or 1 tsp.
   garlic powder
pastry for 10" one-crust pie

Wrap bacon around partridge and simmer in sherry over medium heat for 45 minutes or until tender. Remove meat from bones and dice. Add to vegetables and mix thoroughly. Pour mixture and juices into a greased 10" pie pan. Cover with pastry and pierce with a fork. Bake at 350 degrees for 1 hour 45 minutes.

8 servings

Much better in this pie than in a pear tree.

Minnesota

Roast Wild Duck

salt
2 wild ducks
salt and pepper
2 T. soft butter
1 orange, cut in small pieces
2 stalks celery, diced
1 apple, diced
1 medium onion, diced
4-6 bacon strips
2 c. cooked wild rice

Rub salt in cavity of ducks and rinse thoroughly with cold water. Clean ducks well, removing all pin feathers, and salt and pepper them in and out. Mix butter with orange, celery, apple and onion. Stuff in cavities and close. Prick skin on breasts so fat will drain. Place breast side up on rack in greased casserole or pan. Put 2 or 3 strips of bacon on each duck. Roast covered at 275 degrees for 3 hours or until tender. Remove sections of meat from bone and place on bed of cooked wild rice.

4 servings

For the ducks unlimited that never reach the mantelpiece.

German

Hasenpfeffer

Rabbit

1½ c. cider vinegar
1½ c. cold water
½ c. sugar
3 bay leaves
2 tsp. salt
1 tsp. whole cloves
¼ tsp. pepper
1/8 tsp. allspice
1 medium onion, sliced
2-3 lb. young rabbit, cut in pieces
½ c. flour
butter or shortening
crushed gingersnaps or flour for
thickening

Combine vinegar, water, sugar, spices, seasonings and onion in a large glass bowl. Add rabbit pieces. Cover and refrigerate for at least 12 hours; preferably 1-2 days. Remove rabbit and drain well; reserving marinade. Coat pieces in flour and brown well in ¼" hot butter or shortening in a heavy skillet. Remove excess drippings and add strained marinade. Heat to boiling, reduce heat to low, cover and simmer until fork tender, about 1 hour or longer. Remove rabbit meat to warm platter. Thicken liquid with crushed gingersnaps for gravy to serve over rabbit.

4-6 servings

Mexican

Huevos Rancheros

Ranch-Style Eggs

2 T. vegetable oil
¼ c. chopped onion
1 clove garlic, minced
1 (16 oz.) can tomatoes with juice,
chopped (2 c.)
1 c. canned tomato sauce
1 tsp. salt
1 tsp. chili powder
½ tsp. sugar
¼ tsp. pepper
6-8 eggs
vegetable oil for frying
6-8 tortillas

Heat 2 tablespoons oil in a 10" skillet. Add onion and garlic, cook until onion is soft, about 5 minutes. Add tomatoes, tomato sauce, salt, chili powder, sugar and pepper; stir thoroughly and bring to a boil. Reduce heat and simmer about 10 minutes, stirring occasionally. Break eggs carefully into simmering sauce; poach 3-4 minutes or until yolks start to set, occasionally spooning a little sauce over eggs as they cook.

Meanwhile, heat about ¼" oil in another skillet; fry tortillas until brown on both sides; drain on paper towels. To serve, place each warm tortilla on a plate, spoon some sauce over and top with poached egg. Mexican Salsa (canned or see index) and tomato sauce in equal parts may be substituted for the sauce recipe.

6-8 servings

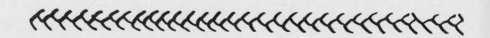

French
Eggs Provencale

1 small onion, chopped
1-2 cloves garlic, minced
2 T. olive oil
1 (16 oz.) can Italian-style plum
  tomatoes, chopped
½ tsp. each thyme, oregano and
  basil
4 eggs
salt
4 slices French bread, buttered
  and fried
minced parsley

In 7" skillet, saute onion and
garlic in olive oil until golden.
Add tomatoes and herbs. Simmer
covered 10 minutes. With the
back of a tablespoon, make four
"nests" in the tomato mixture and
gently break an egg into each
indentation. Sprinkle with salt
and cover to poach eggs gently 7-
10 minutes, as desired. Place egg
and sauce on fried French bread
slices. Sprinkle with parsley.

4 servings

Brazilian
Panqueca de Legume

Vegetable Pancakes

2 eggs
2 c. milk
2 c. flour
¼ tsp. salt
vegetable oil for frying
5-6 small potatoes, chopped fine
1 c. cut-up green beans, fresh or
  frozen
2 large carrots, finely chopped
1 tsp. salt
1 tsp. chopped parsley
½ lb. bacon, chopped
3 hard-cooked eggs, finely
  chopped
½ c. shredded Cheddar cheese
1 c. sour cream
grated Parmesan cheese

Mix eggs, milk, flour and ¼ teaspoon salt together to form crepe
batter. Chill at least 45 minutes.
Oil a crepe pan and fry crepes one
at a time. These can be done
ahead and kept with waxed paper
between each one in refrigerator
or freezer.

To complete, cover chopped
potatoes, beans and carrots with
water; add 1 teaspoon salt and
cook on medium heat 15 minutes
or until tender. Drain through a
sieve, sprinkle parsley over vegetables and let cool. Fry the bacon
lightly until transparent. Add the
bacon and a little of the fat to the
cooled vegetable mixture. Stir
well. Divide vegetable stuffing
among the crepes. Mix the eggs
and cheese together and sprinkle
over stuffing. Roll crepe and place
seam side down in 9" x 13"
greased glass baking dish. Spread
sour cream over crepes. Sprinkle
liberally with Parmesan cheese.
Bake 20 minutes at 350 degrees.

12 servings

American
Cheese and Crab Pie

Swiss
Cheese Fondue

1 c. shredded natural Swiss cheese
   (4 oz.)
9" unbaked pie shell
1 (7½ oz.) can crab meat, drained
   and flaked (or 8 oz. frozen)
2 green onions, chopped,
   including tops
3 eggs, beaten
1 c. light cream
½ tsp. grated lemon rind
½ tsp. salt
¼ tsp. dry mustard
dash of mace (optional)
¼ c. sliced almonds
parsley

Arrange cheese in pie shell and
top with crab meat. Sprinkle with
green onions. Mix eggs, cream,
lemon rind, salt, dry mustard and
mace. Pour evenly over crab and
top with sliced almonds. Bake in
325 degree oven for 1 hour or
until set. Remove from oven and
let stand for 10 minutes before
serving. Garnish with parsley.

6-8 servings

1 clove garlic, peeled and cut in
   half
2½-3 c. dry white wine
14 oz. Emmenthal cheese, finely
   grated
14 oz. Gruyere cheese, finely
   grated
1 tsp. lemon juice
1 tsp. cornstarch
1 oz. Kirsch
pinch of baking soda
nutmeg
crusty French bread, cut in 1"
   cubes

Prepare fondue in earthenware
crock (Caquelon) or very heavy
enamel saucepan on the stove.
Rub crock with garlic. Heat wine
and add cheese, stirring slowly on
low heat in "figure 8" pattern
without touching bottom of the
crock. When cheese is melted,
while stirring add lemon juice,
cornstarch, Kirsch and soda; heat
until bubbly. Sprinkle with nutmeg and place crock on alcohol
burner at serving table. Spear
bread cubes with fondue fork and
swirl in cheese. A crust will form
on the bottom of the crock. This
should be removed, cut into pieces and served.

4 servings

*Extra special when served with
chilled white wine and crisp salad.*

Minnesota
Wild Rice Casserole

1 c. uncooked wild rice
½ c. butter
½ lb. mushrooms, sliced
2 T. minced onion
2 T. minced green pepper
1 clove garlic, minced
¼ c. chopped pecans
3 c. chicken broth
salt and pepper to taste

Wash and soak wild rice 1 hour in boiling water or soak overnight. Melt butter and add mushrooms, onion, green pepper and garlic. Cook 5 minutes, stirring often. Add pecans and cook 1 minute more. Drain rice and add to mushroom mixture. Add broth, salt and pepper. Pour into a 1½-quart greased casserole. Cover and bake in a 325 degree oven for 1 hour, then uncover and continue baking 20-25 minutes.

6-8 servings

Add leftover chicken or turkey and it's a main course.

Vietnamese
Com Rang

Fried Rice

3 T. vegetable oil
1 c. finely chopped broccoli
2 eggs, lightly beaten
2-3 c. cooked white rice
1 c. diced cooked ham
1 tsp. brown sugar
1 tsp. soy sauce
½ tsp. salt
½ tsp. pepper
½ tsp. garlic powder

Heat wok until very hot and add 1 tablespoon oil. Stir-fry broccoli just until tender-crisp; remove. Clean and dry wok. Heat again and add 2 tablespoons oil. Add eggs, stirring with a spatula for approximately 2 minutes. Add broccoli and remaining ingredients. Stir-fry until hot.

2-4 servings

North African
Couscous

A Rice-like Dish

2 T. butter
1 c. couscous or semolina
1 c. boiling water or broth
pinch of salt
¼ tsp. cayenne, red or chili
    pepper powder (optional)

Melt butter in a medium saucepan. Add couscous and mix carefully, coating all the grains with butter. Add boiling water and salt and cover. Remove from heat; let stand 15 minutes. May add additional seasonings. Stir with fork to separate grains before serving. Use instead of rice with poultry or meat. Also good with stew mixed through it.

4 servings

Traditionally this is steamed in a perforated pan called a couscousier, but this easy method produces similar results.

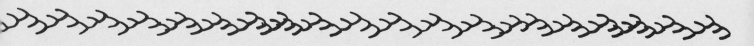

East Indian
Pulao

Seasoned Rice and Peas

1 large onion, thinly sliced
½ c. butter
2-1/8 c. uncooked white rice (1 lb.)
4 c. water
2 chicken bouillon cubes
1 T. salt
1 tsp. curry powder
1/8 tsp. each cayenne, ginger, black pepper and tumeric
½ tsp. cumin
1 (10 oz.) pkg. frozen peas, thawed

In heavy saucepan, saute onion in ¼ cup butter until clear. Add rice and saute approximately 5 minutes. Pour in water. Add bouillon cubes, salt, curry powder and remaining seasonings; stir to mix. Cover tightly and simmer slowly, without stirring, for 25 minutes. Remove cover and place peas and remaining butter on top. Cover and cook slowly for 5 minutes or until peas are tender. Mix lightly and serve.

8 servings

A nice spicy rice.

Italian
Broccoli Linguine

1 lb. Italian linguine
3 oz. olive oil
4 cloves garlic, mashed or minced
1 large bunch broccoli, finely chopped, including 1"-2" of stems
¾ c. chopped walnuts
½ c. sliced pitted black olives
salt
freshly ground pepper
3 oz. grated Romano or Parmesan cheese

Cook linguine according to package directions until "al dente" (tender but not mushy); drain. Heat olive oil in large skillet and saute garlic until golden. Add chopped broccoli, walnuts and olives; cook and stir over moderate heat until very hot. Season to taste. Pour over hot linguine. Sprinkle grated cheese on top and serve immediately.

6 servings

Sounds good, tastes even better.

Hungarian
Cabbage Noodles

1 (10 oz.) pkg. wide egg noodles
1 large head cabbage
1 T. salt
1 medium onion, chopped
¼ c. butter
1 tsp. paprika
1 tsp. oregano
½ tsp. coarse pepper
¼ c. snipped parsley
salt to taste

Boil noodles following directions on package and drain. Finely chop cabbage and wash in colander. Sprinkle 1 tablespoon salt over cabbage, mix and let stand for 10 minutes. Meanwhile, saute onion in butter until golden and sprinkle with paprika. Squeeze cabbage with hands until dry. Add to onion in skillet, mix well and continue cooking over medium heat for 15 minutes, stirring often to prevent scorching. Stir in cooked noodles and seasonings until well blended. Can be reheated.

8-10 servings

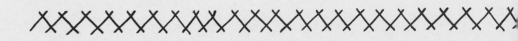

Italian
Noodles Alfredo

Eastern European
Pierogi

Filled Pocket Noodles

1 lb. wide noodles
¼ lb. unsalted butter
1 T. olive oil
½ c. cream
¾ c. grated fresh Parmesan
  cheese
1 egg, lightly beaten
1 (8 oz.) can clams (optional)

Cook and drain noodles. Melt
butter in a saucepan and add oil.
Slowly add cream, cheese and
egg, stirring until mixture begins
to thicken. Do not boil. Mix noodles and sauce lightly. Sprinkle
with additional cheese, if desired.
Serve immediately. Drained
clams may be added to the sauce
for variety.

4-6 servings

Loved the world over!

Dough:
2 c. flour
1 whole egg plus 1 yolk
¼ tsp. salt (scant)
2 T. sour cream
1 tsp. butter for a richer dough
  (optional)
Filling choices, see below

Mix ingredients and knead into
soft pliable dough. Roll thin on
board. Cut into 2″ squares. Place
a small spoonful of filling a little
to one side of each square. Fold
over and pinch edges together
into triangle shape. Boil carefully
in salted water about 5 minutes
and remove with slotted spoon.
Serve with melted butter or
"skwarki" (shredded fried bacon
in butter).

6-8 servings

Pierogi Filling Choices:

Cheese and Potato Filling:
1 c. mashed potatoes
1 c. dry cottage cheese
2 T. chives or green onions,
  minced
salt and pepper to taste

Mix ingredients thoroughly, but
lightly and fill dough squares as
directed.

Prune or Ripe Plum Filling:
1 c. prunes or ripe plums
1 T. sugar
1 tsp. lemon juice
whipped cream

Soak prunes in water overnight.
Add sugar, cook until tender and
add lemon juice. When cool,
remove pits and fill Pierogi; or pit
plums and fill cavity with cube of
sugar dipped in cinnamon. Fill
dough squares and serve with
whipped cream.

A Polish and Ukranian favorite.

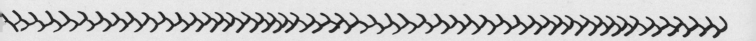

Jewish
Kugel

Fruited Noodle Pudding

½ lb. medium wide noodles (8 oz.)
4-5 medium apples, peeled and diced (3 c.)
¼ lb. butter
1½ c. sour cream (12 oz.)
¾ c. seedless raisins
3 T. sugar
1 tsp. cinnamon
2 T. poppy seeds (optional)
3 eggs, beaten

Cook noodles according to directions on package; drain. Saute apples in butter until slightly soft. Combine apples with cooked noodles; add remaining ingredients and stir gently. Place in 9" x 9" buttered pan. Cover with foil and refrigerate overnight. Bake covered at 350 degrees for 30 minutes. Uncover and continue baking at 375 degrees for 30 more minutes. Cut into squares and serve warm.

10-12 servings

Often called lucshen kugel.

Jewish
Kreplach

Filled Noodle Dough

Dough:
1 egg
¾ c. flour
½ eggshell of warm water
½ tsp. salt

Meat Filling:
1½ lb. cooked lean pot roast
1 egg
1 small onion, finely chopped
1 T. schmaltz, rendered chicken fat (see index)
salt and pepper to taste

Cheese Filling:
2 c. pressed dry cottage cheese
1 egg
2 T. sour cream
salt and pepper to taste

To make dough, mix 1 egg, flour, water and ½ tsp. salt; let stand for 30 minutes. For meat filling, grind pot roast and add 1 egg. Saute chopped onion in schmaltz and add to meat mixture with salt and pepper. For cheese filling, combine ingredients.

To make the kreplach, roll out dough until thin and cut into 2" squares. Place ½ teaspoon of either filling in center and fold into triangles. Pinch edges to seal. Lift two corners and pinch together on top. Drop into lightly salted boiling water and cook until they float like dumplings. Meat kreplach may then be served in soup or fried and served as a side dish. Cheese kreplach may also be fried if desired following boiling and served with sour cream and jam.

Yield 2-2½ dozen

First cousin to pierogi.

Jewish
Cottage Cheese Noodle Puddings

1 (1 lb.) pkg. noodles
4 eggs
1 (16 oz.) carton cream-style
    cottage cheese
½ c. sour cream
½ tsp. salt
½ c. sugar
1 tsp. cinnamon
¼ c. butter
½ c. light corn syrup

Cook noodles in rapidly boiling water about 9-12 minutes or until tender. Drain and mix with eggs, cottage cheese, sour cream and salt. Mix sugar and cinnamon and add half of it to noodles. Spoon into greased cupcake tins and dot generously with butter and remaining cinnamon-sugar. Bake at 350 degrees for 20-30 minutes or until done. Remove to cookie sheet, drizzle with syrup and return to oven for 5 minutes to glaze and crisp.

Yield 2 dozen

Nice individual molds to surround a roast.

Eastern European
Vareniki

Filled Dumplings

2 whole eggs plus 1 yolk
¾ c. cold water
1 tsp. salt
1 T. vegetable oil
3-4 c. flour

Potato Filling:
2 lb. small red potatoes
½ lb. sharp Cheddar cheese,
    shredded
1 large onion, chopped
¼ c. butter
¼ c. additional butter for topping

Beat eggs and egg yolk until foamy. Add water, salt and oil. Gradually add 3 cups flour (more may be needed to achieve workable consistency). Knead in bowl until pliable. Let stand covered for about ½ hour.

Boil potatoes for filling and drain. Peel and mash until smooth. Add cheese to hot mashed potatoes. Saute onion in ¼ cup butter; add to mixture and blend well.

Roll dough out on well-floured board to 1/8" thickness and cut in 2"-3" rounds with cookie cutter. Place 1 tablespoon of filling in center of each round, fold over and press edges together tightly. Drop into vigorously boiling water. Cook 2-3 minutes after water comes to boil again. Remove with slotted spoon and drain well to prevent sticking. Let cool. Melt butter and pour evenly over Vareniki. The cheese filling for Kreplach (see index) also may be used.

Yield 5 dozen

German
Spaetzle

Tiny Egg Dumplings

1 c. flour
1 egg
½ tsp. salt
½ c. milk
6 c. water with 1 tsp. salt

Mix flour, egg and salt in bowl. Pour in milk gradually, stirring until smooth and thin, like pancake batter. Bring salted water to a boil in a large saucepan or pot. Drop small bits of batter from a teaspoon or press through a coarse colander into boiling water and boil rapidly 8-10 minutes. Drain, rinse with hot water, drain again. Serve in soup or with roast or sauerbraten. Especially good with fine bread crumbs and melted butter on top.

Yield about 2 cups

A cross between a curly noodle and a small dumpling.

Norwegian
Klub

Potato Dumplings

¼ lb. salt pork
3 qt. water
4 c. grated uncooked potatoes
3 c. flour
1 tsp. salt
1 tsp. baking powder
melted butter

Parboil salt pork for 40 minutes in water. Remove and cut into small pieces. Save the pork broth. Mix potatoes, flour, salt and baking powder. Form into balls about the size of an apple and press 3 pieces of salt pork into center of each ball. Roll lightly in flour and drop into simmering pork broth. Simmer covered for about 45 minutes or until dumplings are tender. Remove from broth and serve with melted butter poured over the top. Leftover dumplings may be sliced and fried in butter.

Yield 10-15 dumplings

In Sunburg and Kerkhoven, Minnesota, they serve Klub on certain days of the week. Check the days and plan a trip.

Italian
Gnocci de Negris

Cheese Dumplings

1 c. flour
1 c. fresh ricotta cheese
salt and pepper to taste

Mix flour and cheese thoroughly together. With hands, roll out dough into thin "logs" about ½" thick. Cut each roll into 1" pieces. (The pieces will look like little pillows.) Place index finger in middle of each piece, push down to form a dent or "dimple." Drop gently into boiling salted water and cook until tender, 8-10 minutes; drain. Season to taste with salt and pepper. Serve covered with hot Marinara Sauce (see index) and grated cheese.

4 servings

Could be a distinctive luncheon dish.

XXXXXXXXXXXXXXXXXXXXXXXXXXXXXXXXXXX

Kluski

Raw Potato Dumplings

2 c. grated raw potatoes
2 eggs, beaten
1 tsp. salt
2 c. flour
1 medium onion, grated
melted butter
2-3 slices bacon, cut in pieces,
    fried crisp (optional)

Drain off liquid from potatoes. Add eggs, salt, flour and onion to make stiff dough. Drop into salted boiling water from wet tablespoon, dipped in boiling water. Boil 15-20 minutes. Dumplings should be 1½" long and ½" in diameter when cooked. Drain and rinse with cold water. Melt butter in frying pan; add kluski, heat and serve. Fried bacon pieces may be added to the butter, if desired.

4 servings

Potato Pancakes

2 c. grated raw potatoes (2 large)
1 medium onion, grated
2 eggs, beaten
3 T. flour
1 tsp. salt
½ tsp. pepper
½ tsp. baking powder
vegetable oil for frying
applesauce
sour cream

Mix potatoes thoroughly with onion, eggs, flour, salt, pepper and baking powder. Heat oil ¼" deep in large skillet. Drop potato batter from tablespoon into pan and flatten. Let fry until crisp and brown before turning to brown on other side. Remove and drain on paper towels. Serve hot with applesauce or sour cream. These can be made ahead and reheated in the oven.

Yield 1 dozen

Carrot Mold

½ c. brown sugar, tightly packed
½ c. vegetable shortening
pinch of salt
2 eggs, separated
1 c. flour
1 tsp. baking soda
½ tsp. baking powder
½ tsp. vanilla
½ tsp. almond extract
1 T. water
2 c. grated raw carrots

Cream brown sugar, shortening and salt. Add egg yolks. Beat egg whites until stiff and refrigerate. Sift together flour, soda and baking powder; add to creamed mixture. Add vanilla, almond extract and water. Stir in grated carrots and fold in egg whites. Spread batter evenly in a lightly greased 5-cup ring mold. Bake at 350 degrees for 35-40 minutes. Unmold and serve warm.

8-10 servings

An excellent meat accompaniment with the consistency of moist cake.

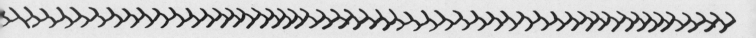

Estonian

Estonian Sauerkraut

New England

Boston Baked Beans

2 T. butter or margarine
1 qt. sauerkraut, rinsed
½ head cabbage, shredded
1 large onion, chopped and
    sauteed in butter
15 dried prunes
2 red apples, peeled, cored and
    sliced
¾ c. sugar
1 T. salt
1 c. water

Place all ingredients in large
saucepan. Cover and cook over
medium heat, stirring occasionally, for about 1½ hours. (To avoid
odor during cooking, cover the
sauerkraut with a piece of black
bread.) Chill and serve.

6-8 servings

*One whiff, you'll know what's
cooking.*

2 lb. navy beans
1 tsp. baking soda
1 lb. salt pork
1 medium onion
⅔ c. dark molasses
2 tsp. dry mustard
4 tsp. salt
½ tsp. pepper
½ c. sugar

Cover beans with cold water and
soak overnight. Drain, put in a
large kettle and cover with cold
water. Add baking soda. Bring to
a boil and simmer for 10 minutes.

Drain and rinse with cold water.
Dice the salt pork into small
pieces. Put ½ of the pork in the
bottom of a 2 quart bean pot
along with the whole onion. Add
the beans and put the remaining
salt pork on top. Mix the remaining ingredients together and add 2
cups of hot water. Pour over the
beans and add enough hot water
to just cover. Cover and bake at
300 degrees for 6 hours, or until
beans are tender and most of the
liquid has been absorbed.
Remove onion before serving.

12-16 servings

Enjoyed in the Midwest too.

the good earth

vegetables & salads

American
Asparagus Loaf

1 c. coarsely crumbled saltine
   crackers
4 T. melted butter
2 eggs, lightly beaten
2 c. milk
½ tsp. salt
dash of pepper
1 tsp. grated onion
2 (10 oz.) pkg. frozen cut
   asparagus, cooked and drained

Saute crackers in butter until
golden brown. Combine eggs,
milk, salt, pepper and onion; mix
well. Add cooked asparagus and
crackers. Place in well-buttered
5" x 9" x 3" loaf pan. Bake at 350
degrees for 30 minutes or until a
knife inserted 1" from edge of pan
comes out clean.

8 servings

Scandinavian
Rodkøl

Red Cabbage

1 head red cabbage (2-3 lb.)
¼ c. butter or margarine
2 medium yellow onions,
   chopped
2 cloves garlic, mashed
4 medium tart apples, sliced
¼ tsp. allspice
2 tsp. salt
½ tsp. pepper
2 T. red wine vinegar
¼ c. water
3-4 T. sugar
1½ c. dry red wine

Shred cabbage; add butter and
saute in heavy oven-proof skillet
or roaster over medium heat for 5
minutes. Add onions, garlic,
apples, allspice, salt and pepper.
Toss together for a few minutes,
then add vinegar, water, sugar
and wine. Cover and bake in 375
degree oven for 1 hour, adding
more wine if needed. Serve with
pork, goose or meatballs.

6-8 servings

*Many nationalities include red
cabbage in their menus.*

Pot Eten Watch Pots

White Cabbage and Beans

1½ lb. navy beans
1 medium head cabbage, separate
    leaves
6 medium potatoes, peeled and
    cubed
1 tsp. salt
5½ T. shortening

Soak beans overnight in a large
pot. Cook in the same water until
done, then add cabbage leaves
and bring to a boil. Simmer vigorously for 30 minutes. Add potatoes, salt and shortening. Cook
for 30 minutes or until potatoes
are very soft. Mash and serve.

6-8 servings

Green Beans with Sour Sauce

4 qt. water
3 tsp. salt
2 lb. fresh green beans (leave
    whole)
2 eggs
½ c. malt vinegar
2 tsp. light brown sugar
½ tsp. dry hot English mustard

In large saucepan, bring 4 quarts
water and 2 teaspoons salt to boil
over high heat. Drop in beans, a
handful at a time, bring water
back to a boil and cook 10-15
minutes or until beans are tender
but still firm. Promptly drain and
keep warm in covered serving
dish.

    Combine eggs, vinegar, sugar,
mustard and 1 teaspoon salt. Beat
vigorously with wire whisk until
smooth. Transfer to top of double
boiler over simmering water. Beat
for 2-3 minutes or until sauce
thickens and coats the whisk.
Pour sauce over beans and serve.

8 servings

Dandelion Greens

2 lb. dandelion greens
boiling water
½ tsp. salt
1 T. butter
salt and pepper to taste

Pick young dandelions before
they blossom as they become bit-
ter after that time. Cut off the
roots and pick the greens over
carefully. Wash well in several
water rinses. Place in kettle and
add a little boiling water. Boil
until tender. Add ½ teaspoon salt
to water just before cooking is
completed. When done, lift greens
into colander, press to drain off
all the water and chop. Add butter, salt and pepper to taste.

4-6 servings

*Forget spraying these weeds — cook
them instead.*

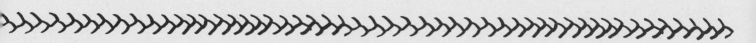

Israeli
Givetch

Mixed Cooked Vegetable

1 onion, chopped
3 T. vegetable oil
2 eggplant, cubed
2 zucchini, cubed
2 green pepper, cubed
3 tomatoes, cut into small pieces
1 tsp. salt
½ tsp. pepper
4 cloves garlic, minced

In a saucepan, fry the onion in oil until golden. Add the remaining ingredients, cover and simmer about 1½ hours. Remove cover and simmer another ½ hour or until all water has cooked from the vegetables.

6-8 servings

A nice way to use the fresh garden produce.

Russian
Morkov

Carrots

1 large onion, chopped
¼ c. cooking oil
4-5 medium carrots, coarsely shredded
4-5 medium parsnips, coarsely shredded
1 T. sugar
1 large green pepper, chopped
1 (8 oz.) can tomato sauce
salt and pepper to taste

Saute onion in oil until limp. Add remaining ingredients and cook over low heat until vegetables are tender, stirring frequently. Serve hot.

4-6 servings

American Indian
Frypan Corn

2 c. kernels fresh sweet corn, cut off cob
½ c. butter
½ c. water
1 T. sugar
salt and pepper to taste

Fry corn in butter over low heat for 10 minutes. Add water, sugar and seasonings and simmer for 5-8 minutes more.

4 servings

A neat way to serve corn to the kids who have lost their two front teeth.

Israeli
Mideastern Eggplant

French
Pommes de Terre Anna

Southern
Sweet Potato Pone

2 large eggplant
2 tsp. salt
½ c. flour
½ c. water
2 eggs
vegetable oil
salt and pepper
1 clove garlic, minced

Sauce:
4 medium tomatoes
1 hot chili pepper
4 tsp. sugar
½ tsp. salt
1 clove garlic, minced

Wash and dry unpeeled eggplant. Slice into ½" thickness. Sprinkle with salt and set aside. Mix flour, water and eggs for batter. Dip eggplant in batter and fry in hot oil. Arrange slices in a casserole and season with salt, pepper and garlic.

Put sauce ingredients in a blender and blend well. Pour into pan and bring to boil; cool. Cover the eggplant with sauce and bake at 350 degrees for 30 minutes. May be served hot or cold.

4-6 servings

6 medium-large potatoes
¼ lb. melted butter or margarine
½ tsp. prepared French mustard
salt and pepper

Select a 9" pan about 2½" deep and butter well. Pare and slice potatoes thinly and brush the slices with butter into which the mustard has been worked.

Arrange the slices around the edge of the pan and cover the bottom, overlapping the slices. Sprinkle with salt and pepper. Continue to build up the layers this way until the pan is filled. If any butter remains, pour over the top. Press the layers down so that the pan is well filled. Bake in 400 degree oven until the slices are tender when tested with a sharp knife, 40-50 minutes.

Remove from oven and let stand a minute or two. Then run a knife around edge of the pan, invert and unmold the golden brown potatoes on hot serving plate.

8 servings

6 medium sweet potatoes
2 c. brown sugar
½ c. melted butter or margarine
½ tsp. nutmeg
½ tsp. allspice
1 c. light or dark molasses
6 eggs, lightly beaten
2 T. flour
1 c. milk
½ tsp. cloves

Peel and grate potatoes. Mix with rest of the ingredients. Bake uncovered in a large greased casserole, at 350 degrees for 1½ hours or until slightly brown on top.

6-8 servings

This sweet vegetable dish is often used as a dessert.

Finnish
Rutabaga Casserole

American Indian
Indian Squash

Korean
Ho-Bak Jan

Fried Zucchini

2 medium rutabagas, peeled and
    diced (about 6 c.)
¼ c. fine dry bread crumbs
¼ c. half and half cream
½ tsp. nutmeg
1 tsp. salt
2 eggs, beaten
3 T. butter

Cover and cook the rutabagas in
salted water until soft, about 20
minutes. Drain and mash. Soak
the bread crumbs in the cream
and stir in nutmeg, salt and beat-
en eggs. Combine with the
mashed rutabagas.

    Turn into a buttered 2½ quart
casserole, dot top with butter and
bake in a 350 degree oven for 1
hour or until lightly browned.

6-8 servings

*This is an old traditional Christmas
dish. Best served with meat.*

1 large winter squash
2 tsp. sugar
½ tsp. salt
3 T. soft butter
1½ tsp. water
3 T. light or dark molasses

Cook halved and seeded squash
in salt water about 20 minutes.
Place halves in baking dish. Make
mixture of other ingredients, fill
squash and bake in a 350 degree
oven until tender.

2 servings

1 large zucchini, washed
1 tsp. salt
1 egg, beaten
1 tsp. sugar
3 T. flour
3 T. oil

Sauce:
3 T. soy sauce
1½ T. vinegar
1 tsp. sugar

Cut zucchini into ¼" slices.
Sprinkle with salt; let stand a few
minutes, wipe dry. Beat egg lightly with sugar. Dredge zucchini
with flour and dip in beaten egg.
Fry in oil until light brown on
both sides. Drain on paper towels. Mix sauce ingredients together and use as a dip for zucchini.

    Other vegetables such as car-
rots, eggplant and onion also may
be prepared this way.

4 servings

Chinese
Zucchini with Oyster Sauce

1 lb. zucchini, unpeeled
3 T. vegetable oil
¼ c. chicken broth
2 tsp. cornstarch
3 tsp. oyster sauce
2 green onions, cut in 2″ lengths, including green tops

Cut zucchini in half lengthwise and slice ¼″ diagonally. Heat wok or pan until hot, add oil and zucchini. Stir-fry for 1 minute. Mix chicken broth with cornstarch and add to zucchini. Stir until well mixed. Add oyster sauce and green onions and stir-fry for ½ minute. If needed, thicken by adding a little more cornstarch and water.

4 servings

Zucchini with a new flavor.

American
Zucchini Casserole

1½ lb. zucchini
water for boiling
2 eggs, lightly beaten
⅓ c. shredded Swiss cheese
½ c. heavy cream
2 T. cornstarch
salt to taste

Cut unpeeled zucchini in 2″ pieces. Cover halfway with water and cook until tender. Drain and place in generously buttered 1½ quart casserole. Break up zucchini with a fork. Add eggs and cheese. Mix together. Blend cream and cornstarch and add to zucchini mixture. Salt to taste. Bake in a 400 degree oven for 20 minutes or until edges and top are slightly brown.

8 servings

Southern
Black-eyed Pea Salad

1 lb. dried black-eyed peas
4-6 oz. water to cover
½ lb. salt pork or bacon, in one chunk
1 onion, studded with 4 cloves
1 bay leaf
½ c. diced onion
¼ c. diced celery
1 T. diced pimiento
2 T. diced green pepper

Dressing:
1 c. vegetable oil
½ c. wine vinegar
¼ tsp. dry mustard
½ tsp. salt
¼ tsp. pepper

Soak peas overnight in cold water. Drain and put into a large kettle. Cover with fresh water, add the meat, onion and bay leaf. Simmer for 35 minutes or until tender. Drain well. When cool, add diced vegetables. Mix dressing together and pour over pea mixture. Refrigerate for several hours until well chilled. Remove meat, onion and bay leaf and serve cold.

8-10 servings

Mennonite
Hot Dandelion Salad

Australian
Rice Salad

South African
H.R.H. Rice Salad

1 qt. young dandelion greens
1 c. sour cream
1 egg, well beaten
½ tsp. salt
1 tsp. butter
2 tsp. sugar
1 T. vinegar

Trim ends of greens, discarding older leaves. Wash and drain. Mix remaining ingredients in saucepan. Bring slowly to a boil, stirring constantly. Add dandelions. Mix well and serve hot.

4 servings

You can be spiffier and use watercress, especially if your dandelion crop has gone to seed.

2 c. uncooked rice
2 c. boiling water
2 T. vinegar
2 T. vegetable oil
1 tsp. curry powder
1 medium onion, diced
1 green pepper, seeded and diced
1 green apple, unpeeled, cored and diced
½ c. raisins
4 oz. cashew nuts

Cook rice in boiling water until tender but still firm (use directions on package). Rinse in cold water, drain and allow to cool thoroughly. Beat together vinegar, oil and curry powder until frothy. Stir mixture into the cooked rice. Add onion, green pepper, apple, raisins and cashew nuts. Refrigerate for 2 hours. Serve with cold lamb or corned beef.

Yield 3 cups

3 c. cooked brown rice
3 c. chopped peaches
1 c. finely chopped celery
½ c. finely chopped onion
½ c. sunflower seeds
½ c. chopped raisins
2 T. lemon juice
1 tsp. curry powder
1 tsp. soy sauce
1 tsp. honey
3 T. chopped parsley
salt to taste
vegetable oil to moisten

Combine all ingredients in a large bowl and mix thoroughly. Chill well and serve cold.

8-10 servings

Fit for a Queen . . .

Lebanese
Tabbouleh
Cracked Wheat Salad

1 c. fine bulgur (cracked wheat)
hot water for soaking
4 tomatoes, chopped (about 1 lb.)
2 c. chopped green onions
3 c. chopped parsley
¼ c. chopped fresh mint
  (optional)
½ c. olive oil
⅓ c. lemon juice
1¼ tsp. salt
½ tsp. freshly ground pepper

Wash wheat, cover with hot water, let stand 30 minutes. Drain, squeeze dry. Mix together the chopped tomatoes, green onions, parsley and mint. Stir in oil, lemon juice, salt and pepper. Mix in the wheat until well blended; chill. Serve on romaine lettuce leaves as a finger salad, or use a fork if you prefer.

6-8 servings

A favorite from the Middle East, becoming quite popular here.

Danish
Hummersalat
Curried Lobster Salad

1 (6½ oz.) can lobster or frozen
  langostinos, thawed
¼ c. mayonnaise
¼ c. sour cream
1 tsp. lemon juice
½ tsp. curry powder (or more to
  taste)
2 stalks celery, chopped
1 apple, cored and diced
lettuce leaves
2 hard-cooked eggs, quartered

Drain lobster and remove membranes. Combine mayonnaise, sour cream, lemon juice and curry powder; blend until smooth. Add lobster, celery and apple and toss lightly. Arrange on lettuce leaves; garnish with egg wedges.

4 servings

Norwegian
Agurkesalat
Cucumber Salad

3 firm cucumbers (medium-large)
1 T. salt
1 c. cider vinegar
dash of pepper
pinch of dry mustard
½ tsp. salt
1 T. sugar (or more to taste)
4 sprigs fresh dill, finely chopped

Peel cucumbers, thinly slice and place on a platter. Sprinkle with 1 tablespoon salt. Place another platter over cucumbers and weight it down with 2 or 3 cans. After an hour, pour off accumulated water and dry cucumbers in a dish towel.

Mix remaining ingredients except the dill and taste for tartness; if a sweeter taste is desired, add up to ½ tablespoon more sugar. Place cucumbers in a flat dish and cover with sauce. Sprinkle with dill and top with 2 or 3 ice cubes. Refrigerate for 3 hours, drain and serve.

Yield 2-3 cups

Use this cucumber salad as you would pickles. It is especially good with meatballs or torsk.

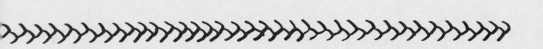

Middle Eastern
Grape-Cucumber Salad

3 c. red, purple or green grapes,
  halved and seeded
1 cucumber, peeled and sliced
4 c. torn or shredded lettuce
1 T. lemon juice
1 T. olive oil
2 tsp. finely chopped fresh mint
  or ½ tsp. dried mint leaves
1 T. chopped fresh dill or ¼ tsp.
  dillweed
¾ tsp. seasoned salt
1 c. plain yogurt or sour cream

Arrange grapes and cucumber on
lettuce in salad bowl. Mix next
five ingredients. Stir into yogurt
and spoon over salad. Watercress
or young spinach leaves may be
substituted for the lettuce.

6 servings

Mexican
Ensalada de Noche Buena

Christmas Eve Salad

¼ c. vegetable oil
2 T. vinegar
2 T. sugar
½ tsp. salt
dash of pepper
2-3 drops Tabasco
juice of one lime
1 head romaine lettuce, washed
1 large apple, peeled, cut into
  pieces
½ c. pineapple chunks, drained
1 banana, sliced
⅓ c. diced beets
¼ c. Spanish peanuts

Combine first seven ingredients in
a bowl, using whisk or fork. Tear
lettuce into pieces and put in a
large bowl. Add remaining ingredients except peanuts and toss
with dressing. Garnish with
peanuts.

6-8 servings

*Different and tasty day or eve the
year around.*

Swedish
Potatissallad

Potato Salad

6 cold, boiled medium potatoes,
  sliced
2 T. chopped onion
2 T. chopped parsley
2 T. chopped chives
2 T. chopped capers
½ c. diced pickled beets

Dressing:
2 T. wine vinegar
6 T. olive or vegetable oil
1 tsp. salt
¼ tsp. pepper

Arrange potato slices in salad
bowl. Place onion, parsley,
chives, capers and beets in rows
on top. Mix dressing ingredients
and pour over potatoes. Chill 1-2
hours. Toss once or twice before
serving.
  Pieces of matjis herring may be
added to the salad for a main
course meal.

4-6 servings

German

German Potato Salad

French

Crudites Salade

Italian

Italian Salad

8 medium potatoes
6 slices bacon
¾ c. sugar
2 T. flour
¾ c. cider vinegar
¼ c. water
½ c. sliced onions (optional)

Scrub potatoes and boil in jackets until tender; peel and slice. Dice bacon and fry; reserve ¼ cup bacon grease. Add sugar to bacon grease, stir in flour, slowly adding vinegar and water. Simmer until clear and pour over potatoes. Top with crumbled bacon and sliced onions, if desired.

8 servings

9 spears fresh asparagus, cut in small pieces
¾ c. chopped raw cauliflower
¾ c. chopped raw broccoli
¾ c. slivered celery
1 small zucchini, thinly sliced
½ c. thinly sliced raw mushrooms
1 small cucumber, thinly sliced
4 green onions, thinly sliced
¼ c. thinly sliced radishes
cherry tomatoes

Vinaigrette Dressing:
1½ c. oil
½ c. white wine vinegar
2 tsp. salt
¼ tsp. pepper
½ tsp. sugar
¼ tsp. ground rosemary

Place all vegetables in a bowl and toss. Blend ingredients for dressing and pour over raw vegetables. Refrigerate for 1 hour or longer.

Yield 2 cups

3 medium tomatoes, peeled and chopped
2 cucumbers, peeled and chopped
2 c. sliced celery
½ c. sliced ripe olives
½ c. chopped green pepper
½ c. chopped green onions
¼ c. broken walnuts

Dressing:
½ c. tarragon vinegar
¼ c. vegetable oil
1 tsp. salt
½ tsp. pepper
½ tsp. oregano

Place all vegetables and nuts in a large bowl. Mix dressing ingredients together and pour over vegetables. Toss well and marinate for 2 hours or longer.

Yield 6 cups

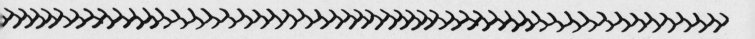

Chinese

Sesame Chicken and Won Ton Salad

2 doz. won ton skins
vegetable oil
1 bunch (¼ lb.) watercress
6 c. shredded iceberg lettuce
1 can (8 oz.) water chestnuts,
    drained and sliced
2 c. cold cooked shredded chicken
    or turkey

Sesame Dressing:
¼ c. vegetable oil
2 T. sesame seed
2½ T. soy sauce
2½ T. white vinegar
1½ T. sugar
¼ tsp. salt

Cut won ton into ½" strips. Heat ¼" oil in frying pan over medium heat. Add won ton strips a few at a time and fry until crisp and golden, about 30 seconds. Remove with a slotted spoon, drain and let cool. Store in airtight container at room temperature if made a day ahead.

Remove tender leaves from stems of watercress, wash and drain. In a large salad bowl, combine watercress leaves, shredded lettuce, water chestnuts and chicken. Cover and chill.

Combine oil and sesame seed in a small frying pan and cook over medium-low heat, stirring occasionally until seeds are golden, about 2 minutes. Let cool. Stir in soy sauce, vinegar, sugar and salt. When serving salad, add fried won ton strips and toss with the sesame dressing.

4 servings

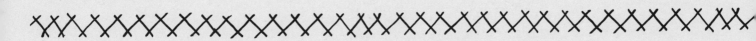

a bit of this & that

potpourri

American

Old-Fashioned Lemonade

2 large lemons
1 medium orange
½ c. sugar
1 qt. cold water
fresh mint leaves

Squeeze lemons and orange. Add sugar, water and mint leaves. Stir well and serve over ice cubes.

4 servings

Great on a hot summer day with memories of the "1¢ lemonade" stand and the screened-in porch.

American

Old-Fashioned Cocoa

¼ c. cocoa
¼ c. sugar
pinch of salt
1 c. water
¼ tsp. vanilla
3 c. milk

Mix cocoa, sugar and salt together in a saucepan. Add water to form paste. Boil for 1 minute. Add vanilla and milk and heat, but do not boil. Serve in cups topped with whipped cream or marshmallows, if desired.

4 servings

This will take you back to the days when cocoa was homemade by Mom, not from the package.

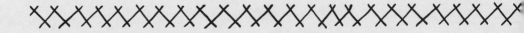

Cranberry Tea

Wassail Punch

Mexican Coffee

1 qt. cranberries
4 qt. water
2½ c. sugar
½ c. cinnamon candies
12 whole cloves
½ tsp. nutmeg
½ tsp. cinnamon
½ tsp. allspice
juice of 3 oranges
juice of 3 lemons

Bring cranberries and 1 quart water to a boil. In another pan, bring 3 quarts water and sugar to boil; add cinnamon candies, cloves and spices and simmer. Put cranberries through a sieve and combine with other liquid. Before serving, add juice of oranges and lemons. Serve hot.

12-15 servings

A winter warmer also good for the holidays.

1 qt. tea
1 qt. cranberry juice
1 qt. apple juice
1 c. sugar
2 c. orange juice
¾ c. lemon juice
3 sticks cinnamon
12 whole cloves

Combine all ingredients in a large pot. Simmer for ½ hour. Remove cinnamon and cloves. Serve warm from a large punch bowl.

18-20 (6 oz.) servings

A lovely tradition at Christmas; surround the bowl with sprigs of holly.

10 c. strong black coffee
1 c. heavy cream
3 T. chocolate sauce
1 c. brandy

Mix coffee, cream, chocolate sauce and brandy in a saucepan and heat. Serve with whipped cream and chocolate shavings, if desired.

Yield 12 cups

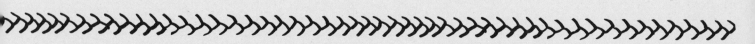

American
Old-Fashioned Buttermilk Pancakes

1 egg
1¼ c. buttermilk
¾ c. flour
½ tsp. salt
½ tsp. baking soda
¼ tsp. sugar
1 T. melted shortening
1½ T. shortening for frying

Beat ingredients except 1½ tablespoons shortening together with a fork in order given. Heat shortening in a heavy pan until hot and drop batter by tablespoonfuls. Turn pancakes over with spatula when bubbles appear. When brown on both sides, remove and serve with maple syrup or strawberry jam.

Yield 3-4 dozen 2″ pancakes

German
Golden Delight Pancakes

1 c. cream-style cottage cheese
6 eggs
¼ c. milk
¼ c. vegetable oil
½ c. flour
¼ tsp. salt
1 c. fresh blueberries or chopped apple

Place all ingredients except fruit in blender. Blend well for 1 minute. Stir the fruit in by hand. Bake on lightly greased griddle using ¼ cup batter per pancake.

4-5 servings

For brunch or breakfast they are "unbeatable."

American Indian
Indian Slapjacks

1 egg, well beaten
1 c. milk
½ c. yellow cornmeal
½ c. flour
½ tsp. salt
shortening, to grease griddle
melted butter
maple syrup

Combine egg and milk; stir into combined cornmeal, flour and salt. Drop batter by tablespoonfuls onto hot greased griddle. Cook until edges are done; turn and cook on other side. Serve with melted butter and maple syrup.

Yield 1½ dozen 4″ slapjacks

Finnish
Kropsu

Baked Pancake

¼ c. butter
2 eggs
2 c. milk
1 c. flour
½ tsp. salt
lingonberry sauce, currant jelly or
   syrup

Melt butter in 8" x 12" x 2" pan.
Break eggs into bowl. Add milk
alternately with flour that has
been sifted with the salt; add
melted butter, making a thin batter. Do not overbeat. Pour batter
into sizzling pan and bake 40
minutes at 400 degrees. Serve hot
with Lingonberry Sauce (see
index), jelly or syrup.

2-4 servings

Swedish
Tjack Pannkaka

Omelet Popover

4 eggs
1½ c. flour
½ tsp. salt
1½ c. milk
¼ c. butter

Beat eggs lightly; add flour and
salt to make stiff dough. Slowly
add milk, while stirring, to make
thin batter. On top of stove, melt
butter in 9" x 12" pan. Pour
batter into pan and bake in 400
degree oven for 30 minutes.
Remove and let cool a few
moments until butter is absorbed.
Serve with cranberries, jelly or
Lingonberry Sauce (see index).
Sausages may be served on the
side for brunch or lunch.

6-8 servings

Swedish
Fläskpannkaka

Oven Pancake with Bacon

¾ c. flour
1 tsp. sugar
salt (optional)
2 eggs
2 c. milk
½ lb. bacon
lingonberries or jam

Sift flour into bowl. Add sugar
and salt. Mix eggs and milk and
add gradually to flour mixture,
stirring until well blended. Dice
bacon and fry in ovenproof 10"
skillet. Drain off some of the fat.
Beat batter, pour over bacon and
bake at 425 degrees for 30 minutes or until set and nicely
browned. Cut in sections and
serve with lingonberries or jam.

4 servings

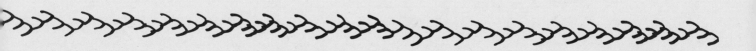

Danish
Aebleskiver

Apple Pancake Balls

3 eggs, separated
2 T. sugar
½ tsp. salt
2 c. buttermilk
2 c. flour
1 tsp. baking soda
1 tsp. baking powder
¾ c. vegetable shortening or
   butter
1 c. applesauce, or 2 apples,
   peeled and thinly sliced
   (optional)
butter, maple syrup, jam or jelly

Beat egg yolks. Add sugar, salt and buttermilk. Sift flour, soda and baking powder together and add to first mixture. Beat egg whites until stiff and fold in batter. Grease each aebleskiver pan depression with shortening. Heat on stove; when hot, fill ⅔ full with batter. Cook until bubbly. Add a teaspoon of applesauce in center and cover with batter. Turn ball carefully with a fork to finish cooking. Remove and serve with butter, maple syrup, jam, jelly or brown sugar. If you don't have an aebleskiver pan, a large frypan may be used. Drop batter by spoonfuls into melted butter and brown on both sides. Top with applesauce.

Yield 4 dozen

It once was customary to turn these in the pan with a knitting needle.

American
Flaky Pie Crust

2 c. sifted flour
1 tsp. salt
½ tsp. baking powder
1 c. vegetable shortening
6-8 T. ice water

Mix the dry ingredients and cut in the shortening slightly. Add 6 tablespoons of ice water and blend with pastry blender or two knives. Add 2 more tablespoons of water if necessary. Form 2 balls, wrap in waxed paper and chill 30 minutes. Roll out on floured pastry cloth to desired size. Repeat with other half. Use as directed for your favorite pie.

Yield 2 crusts

Italian

Thick Sicilian Pizza Crust

4½ c. flour
1 pkg. dry yeast
1½ tsp. salt
1½ c. warm water (110-115 degrees)
2 T. cooking oil

Mix 2 cups flour, yeast and salt. Add water and oil; beat at low speed with electric mixer for ½ minute. Scrape bowl often while mixing. Change to high speed and beat 3 more minutes. Stir in enough remaining flour to make a fairly stiff dough. Knead until smooth on a floured surface. Place dough in a greased bowl and cover with cloth; let rise until double, turning once during rising, approximately 1 hour. Place dough in greased pizza pan, pat down from center to edges of pan. Cover and let rise another 45 minutes.

Top with Pizza Sauce (see index) and bake in 475 degree oven for 25 minutes. Add the toppings of your choice: pepperoni slices, chopped onions, green peppers, mushrooms, olives, sliced cooked sausage, shrimp, ground beef, etc. Cover with shredded Mozzarella cheese, return to oven and bake 10-15 minutes more.

6-8 servings

For deep dish pizza at home.

Canadian

Beer Batter

For Frying Fish

1 c. beer
1 c. flour
1 T. salt
1 tsp. baking soda
2 eggs, beaten
½ tsp. dill weed
6-8 servings of pan fish fillets (walleyes or smelt)

Combine all ingredients except fish. Wipe fish as dry as possible. Dip in batter and fry in deep hot fat, one or two at a time, until golden brown.

Batter improves if made at least 6 hours before use.

Yield 2 cups of batter

American
Corn Dogs

Hot Dogs on a Stick

½ c. yellow cornmeal
1½ c. flour
4 tsp. baking powder
1½ tsp. salt
¼ c. sugar
1 egg, beaten with 1 c. milk
8-10 wieners
8-10 wooden sticks
vegetable oil for deep frying

Mix dry ingredients together; add egg and milk. Place wieners on wooden sticks; dip into batter. Heat oil to 375 degrees; deep fry until golden brown.

Yield 8-10 corn dogs

Fun for the kids to make and eat.

Israeli
Falafel

Chick Pea Croquettes

8 oz. dried chick peas
¼ c. bulgur (cracked wheat)
3 cloves garlic, crushed
1 tsp. salt
3 tsp. cumin
½ tsp. chili pepper
¼ tsp. coriander
1 egg
vegetable oil for deep frying

Soak chick peas for 12 hours and grind coarsely. Soak bulgur for 1 hour and, if coarsely cracked, put through a grinder as well. Mix all ingredients together. Shape into balls, about ¾" in diameter. Deep fry in very hot oil until brown. Place falafel in a pita bread smothered with chopped onion, lettuce, tomatoes, cheese, salt and pepper; drizzle lemon juice and olive oil over the filling.

6-8 servings

The Israeli answer to the American Hot Dog and the Mexican Taco.

Danish
Dumplings

For Soup

½ c. butter
1 c. boiling water
1 c. flour
½ tsp. salt
3 eggs

Melt the butter in boiling water in saucepan. Add flour and cook until it no longer sticks to the pan; cool. Add eggs, one at a time, and beat. Drop by teaspoonfuls into hot soup and cook 15-20 minutes.

4-6 servings

Give an international touch to plain broth.

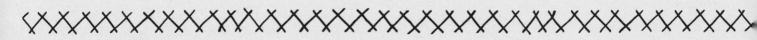

Jewish
Knaidlach

Matzo Balls

2 T. fat (rendered chicken fat or
soft margarine)
2 eggs, lightly beaten
½ c. matzo meal
1 tsp. salt
¼ tsp. sugar
2 T. soup stock or water

Mix fat and eggs together. Add
matzo meal, salt and sugar; blend
well. Add soup stock. Cover
bowl and refrigerate for at least
30 minutes (the longer the batter
is chilled, the easier it is to handle). Bring a large pot of salted
water to a boil. Wet hands, then
shape batter into small balls.
Drop the balls gently into boiling
water; do not crowd. Reduce heat
to moderate, cover and boil for
30-40 minutes. Serve in Chicken
Soup (see index).

Yield 8 matzo balls

A Jewish dumpling.

Slovenian
Noodles

2 eggs
¼ tsp. salt
1½ c. flour

Break eggs into bowl and add
salt. Gradually add flour, stirring
with fork. Form into stiff dough.
Knead on floured board until
smooth. Let stand covered for ½
hour. Divide dough in half and
roll out as thin as possible, using
flour to prevent sticking. Let dry
on cloth spread out on table or
over chairback or cupboard door,
turning several times for even
drying. Fold in half. Roll the sheet
of dried dough jelly roll fashion.
Cut into thin slices, separate and
let dry thoroughly. Store in covered container until ready to use
in soup or casseroles.

Yield 3½ cups

*Memories of noodle day with sheets
of noodles draped over almost every
door in the house would mean
something good in store for dinner,
such as beef noodle soup.*

American
Summer Sausage

2 lb. ground beef (inexpensive
variety)
1 c. water
1 tsp. pepper
½ tsp. garlic salt
½ tsp. dry mustard
1½ tsp. liquid hickory smoke
½ tsp. mace
½ tsp. oregano
3 T. tender quick curing salt

Mix all ingredients together.
Shape into two rolls and wrap in
foil. Refrigerate for 24 hours.
Poke a few holes in foil for drain-
age, put in pan and cover with
boiling water. Cover and boil for
1 hour; remove from water and
drain. Leave in foil and refrigerate
for 24 hours. Slice and serve plain
or in sandwiches.

Yield 2 rolls

*It's great to say you made your own.
Easy too.*

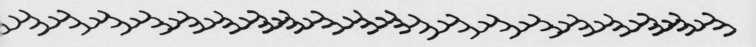

Scottish
Scotch Eggs

6-8 hard-cooked eggs
2 uncooked eggs, beaten
flour
¾ lb. fine grade spicy country-
   style sausage
fine dry bread crumbs
vegetable oil for deep frying

Shell the hard-cooked eggs and
lightly dip them in the beaten
eggs. Roll them in flour and wrap
completely in a thin layer of sausage meat. Brush the sausage with
additional beaten egg and roll in
bread crumbs. Fry in deep fat (375
degrees) for 2-3 minutes or until
the bread crumbs are golden
brown and the sausage firm.
Place in a baking dish and bake at
400 degrees uncovered for 10 minutes. Serve cold.

6-8 servings

*A fun brunch dish, also good sliced
and served for appetizers.*

American
Indian Sauce

1 doz. apples
1 doz. ripe tomatoes
9 medium onions
3 c. sugar
3 c. vinegar
¼ c. salt
1 tsp. each black pepper, dry
   mustard, cinnamon and
   allspice

Peel apples, tomatoes and onions.
Cut into small pieces and mix
together with remaining ingredients. Use blender if desired. Cook
until thickened, using low heat, 4-
5 hours. Pour into sterilized jars
and seal. Use as condiment with
meats.

Yield 10 pints

*Made in the days before Heinz and
Hunt's had ketchup and chili sauce
on every table.*

Italian
Salsa Pizzaiola

Pizza Sauce

3 oz. olive oil
4 cloves garlic, mashed or finely
   chopped
1 onion, minced
8-12 ripe peeled tomatoes, pureed
   in blender or 2 (28 oz.) cans
   Italian tomatoes
1 (6 oz.) can tomato paste
1 tsp. oregano
1 tsp. basil or parsley
2 tsp. brown sugar
pinch of nutmeg
1 tsp. salt
freshly ground pepper

In 3-4 quart saucepan, heat olive
oil and cook garlic and onion
until soft and transparent but not
brown, about 7-8 minutes, stirring constantly. Blend in pureed
tomatoes, tomato paste, oregano,
basil, brown sugar, nutmeg, salt
and a few grindings of black pepper. Bring the sauce to a boil, turn
heat very low and simmer uncovered, stirring occasionally, for
about 1 hour. When done, the
sauce should be thick and fairly
smooth. This sauce is especially
good on top of Pizza Crust (see
index), but may be served with
spaghetti, ravioli and other pasta.

Yield about 1 quart

Mexican
Mexican Salsa

Hot Sauce or Dip

2 tomatoes, peeled and chopped
4 green onions, including tops,
    minced
1 (4 oz.) can green chilies,
    chopped
1 tsp. vegetable oil
salt, pepper, oregano, garlic
    powder to taste

Blend chopped vegetables, add oil
and seasonings. Mix well and use
as needed.

Yield about 1 cup

*This sauce adds a kick to all Mexican
dishes and is also available ready-
made.*

French
Remoulade Sauce

1½ c. mayonnaise
2 T. drained minced capers
⅓ c. minced dill pickles, drained
2 tsp. grated onion
2 tsp. Dijon mustard
2 tsp. each chopped fresh parsley,
    tarragon, chives and chervil or
    1 tsp. each of the same herbs
    dried
1/8 tsp. anchovy paste

Combine all ingredients in the
order given. Serve with fish or
beef.

Yield 2 cups

*A special flavor to add to open-faced
sandwiches. A French twist to a
Scandinavian treat.*

Scandinavian
Mustard Sauce

½ c. plus 2 T. prepared Dijon
    mustard
½ c. plus 2 T. sugar
3 T. chopped fresh dill or 1 T.
    dried
white vinegar

Combine mustard, sugar and dill.
Add white vinegar slowly to consistency of cream dressing. Use
cold as sauce with Gravlaks (see
index).

Yield ¾ cup

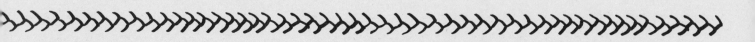

Italian
White Clam Sauce for Pasta

2-3 oz. olive oil
½ c. minced onion
2 cloves garlic, minced
⅓ c. fresh chopped parsley
2 (3 oz.) cans minced clams in
    broth
salt
freshly ground pepper

Heat olive oil in large skillet.
Saute onion and garlic over moderate heat until onion is translucent. Add parsley and clams,
including broth. Cook 5 minutes
over moderately high heat. Salt
and pepper to taste. Pour over
hot cooked pasta, preferably
linguine.

4-6 servings

A gourmet spaghetti creation.

Italian
Marinara Sauce

2-3 oz. olive oil
4 cloves garlic
8-12 ripe tomatoes, peeled and
    pureed, or 2 cans Italian style
    tomatoes, pureed
2 T. brown sugar
½ tsp. oregano
½ tsp. chopped parsley
½ tsp. basil, dried or fresh
pinch of nutmeg
salt and freshly ground pepper
shrimp, clams, mussels (optional)

In large skillet, heat olive oil and
saute garlic cloves until golden
brown. Add pureed tomatoes,
bring to a boil, lower heat and
add brown sugar, oregano, parsley, basil and nutmeg. Cook over
moderately high heat for 20-30
minutes or until reduced to half
original volume. Salt and pepper
to taste. Remove garlic cloves. If
desired, in the last 5-10 minutes of
cooking, add shrimp, clams, mussels or other seafood. Pour over
cooked pasta.

4-6 servings

French
Sauce Vinaigrette

French Dressing

¾ c. olive oil
¼ c. tarragon vinegar
¾ tsp. salt
¼ tsp. freshly ground pepper
2 tsp. minced fresh chives
1/8 tsp. minced chervil
2 tsp. minced capers
1 hard-cooked egg yolk, sieved

Beat all ingredients together and
serve on tossed salad greens or
cold asparagus.

Yield 1 cup

Scandinavian
Lingonberry Sauce

1 qt. lingonberries
1 T. water
1 c. sugar

Rinse lingonberries and simmer with water over low heat until tender. Add sugar and cook until dissolved. Serve plain as a sauce or on pancakes.

Yield 1 quart

American
Chocolate Sauce

2 sq. unsweetened chocolate
½ c. butter or margarine
1½ c. sugar
½ tsp. salt
¾ c. evaporated milk
½ tsp. vanilla

Melt chocolate and butter in top of double boiler over hot water. Stir until chocolate melts. Gradually add sugar and salt while stirring. Blend in milk and cook until mixture is creamy. Remove from heat, stir in vanilla. Serve warm over ice cream or plain cake. Keeps well in refrigerator and can be reheated.

Yield 2 cups

Chocolate lovers beware, this is hard to resist.

American
Homemade Applesauce

4 medium apples
¼-⅓ c. water
1-2 tsp. cinnamon
2-4 T. sugar

Core, pare and quarter apples. Place apples in 1-quart saucepan; add the water and cinnamon. Bring mixture to boil, reduce heat, cover and cook for 10 minutes. Apples should fall apart easily when done. Whip mixture with fork while adding 2 tablespoons sugar. Add more sugar if sweeter taste is desired. Consistency should be smooth. Serve warm or cold.

Yield 1½ cups

They shouldn't fall far from the tree.

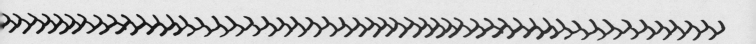

American
Baked Applesauce

Israeli
Techina

Sesame Seed Sauce

French
French Dressing

6 tart cooking apples
juice of 1 small lemon, strained
2 tsp. butter
½ c. sugar (to taste)

Place peeled, cored and quartered apples into a heavy ovenproof saucepan with a tight lid. Coat apples with lemon juice. Cut a circle of waxed paper to fit the saucepan and butter well. Place buttered side on top of apples and cover with lid. Bake at 350 degrees for 45 minutes. When cooked, remove waxed paper and stir in sugar.

Yield 3 cups

A different approach for the orchard crop.

1 c. Tahin (sesame seed paste)
½ c. fresh lemon juice
½ tsp. salt
2 cloves garlic, minced
crushed red pepper to taste
½ tsp. cumin
1-2 tsp. olive oil
coriander or chopped parsley

Place Tahin in bowl of electric mixer, blender or food processor. Add ¼ cup lemon juice slowly until mixture feels thick and grainy. Add ¼ cup more lemon juice until it is thin and smooth. Add water if it is still too grainy. Stir in salt, garlic, red pepper and cumin. Spread on plate. Top with olive oil and coriander in center. Use as a sauce when baking fish or lamb, or thin with water and use as a salad dressing. Adjust seasonings. A few tablespoons of this is used to add flavor to Humus (see index).

Yield 1½ cups

Middle Eastern tang.

⅓ c. vegetable oil
2 T. olive oil
1½ T. red wine vinegar
2½ T. fresh lemon juice
1 tsp. salt
¼ tsp. pepper
1 tsp. sugar
½ tsp. dry mustard
1 clove garlic, peeled and minced
2 scallions, minced
1/8 tsp. thyme, chervil or
   tarragon (optional)

Combine all ingredients in covered jar. Shake before serving. Serve at room temperature.

Yield ⅔ cup

Great on greens.

Minnesota
Blue Cheese Dressing

American
Green Goddess Salad Dressing

American
Horseradish

1 (3-4 oz.) pkg. blue cheese
1-2 T. lemon juice
2 c. mayonnaise
1 (8 oz.) carton sour cream or 1 c. buttermilk
1 clove garlic, minced
salt and freshly ground pepper

Mix cheese with lemon juice to break up the cheese. Blend mayonnaise, sour cream and garlic. Add salt and pepper to taste. Refrigerate in covered container.

Yield 3½ cups

It is a fact that the most famous limestone caves which provide ideal conditions for producing blue-veined cheese are in Roquefort, France. But did you know that near Faribault, Minnesota, sandstone caves are used to ripen an excellent domestic blue cheese?

1 c. mayonnaise
1 clove garlic, minced
3-4 chopped rolled anchovies
¼ c. chopped chives
¼ c. chopped parsley
1 tsp. lemon juice
1 tsp. vinegar
½ tsp. salt
½ tsp. pepper
½ c. sour cream

Mix ingredients together and refrigerate for a few hours. Good with salad of lettuce, diced cucumber and green pepper.

Yield 1¾ cups

This can also be used as a dip for fresh vegetables.

1 lb. fresh horseradish root
2-3 medium red beets
juice of 2 lemons
1 tsp. salt
1 tsp. sugar
2 T. water

Grate horseradish and beets together alternately. (Use care as the horseradish is very strong!) Add lemon juice, salt and sugar to taste. Add water to make it juicy. Serve with Gefilte Fish and Bailik (see index) or roast beef.

Yield 2 pints

Sometimes brings tears to one's eyes.

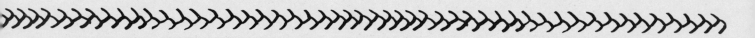

Jewish
Schmaltz

Rendered Chicken Fat

1 lb. chicken fat and skin
¼ tsp. salt
1/8 tsp. pepper
1 medium onion, chopped

Rinse fat in cold water and dice. Place fat and skin in heavy pan and add salt, pepper and chopped onion. Cook uncovered over medium heat for 1 hour or until onions are browned. (The pieces of skin, known as "grebenes," will shrink and crisp and are a great nibble.) Strain to remove browned particles and pour into pint jar. Cool and store in refrigerator. Use in chopped liver and in recipes that call for schmaltz.

Yield 1 pint

An old fashioned flavor that is difficult to replace.

Italian
Italian Carrots

1 lb. carrots, washed and peeled
½ c. vegetable oil
½ c. wine vinegar
1 tsp. sugar
6-8 cloves garlic, chopped very
   coarsely
1½ tsp. oregano, crushed

Cut carrots into strips. Cover with water, bring to a boil and drain immediately. Mix oil, vinegar and sugar in a refrigerator dish with a cover. Add garlic to oil mixture. Add drained carrots and sprinkle with crushed oregano. Mix thoroughly. Refrigerate for several hours or overnight before serving. Stir occasionally while marinating.

The longer this dish is refrigerated, the more the flavor improves. The carrots will keep for weeks. Serve cold as a relish or on an antipasto plate.

Yield 3-4 cups

Carrots are good for your eyes, my dear.

German
Sauerkraut Relish

1 (27 oz.) can sauerkraut
1 onion, diced
1 c. diced celery
1 (2 oz.) jar diced pimiento,
   drained
1 small green pepper, diced
½ tsp. celery seed
¾ c. sugar
½ c. vegetable oil
½ c. white vinegar

Drain sauerkraut thoroughly, squeezing out all liquid; add onion, celery, pimiento, green pepper and celery seed. Set aside. In saucepan, mix sugar, oil and vinegar and bring to boil; cool. Add to sauerkraut mixture and let marinate in refrigerator for 24 hours before serving. Keeps well.

Yield about 5-6 cups

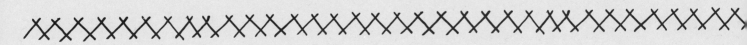

Scottish
Sweet Pepper Relish

Southwestern
Pepper Jelly

American
Sweet Pickles

25 sweet peppers, red and green
12 onions
3 stalks celery
5 c. sugar
2½ pt. vinegar
3 T. salt

Remove seeds from peppers; grind with onions and celery. Cover with boiling water and let stand for 5 minutes; drain. Combine sugar, vinegar and salt. Add pepper mixture and boil for 20 minutes. While hot, seal in pint jars. A good addition to meat loaf (add about 2 tablespoons), or serve with roast beef, hot dogs or hamburgers.

Yield 11-12 pints

2 large red or green peppers
2 large jalapeño peppers (optional)
1 c. white vinegar
3½ c. sugar
3 oz. liquid fruit pectin

Cut and remove seeds from peppers. (If using jalapeño peppers, be careful not to touch seeds, as they cause a burning sensation.) Place peppers and vinegar in a blender or food processor and chop finely. Add this to sugar in a 5-quart pot. Bring to a boil for 3 minutes. Remove from heat and let stand 20 minutes to clear. Skim and remove the heavy pulp from the peppers, stir and return to heat. Boil for 2 more minutes. Remove, add pectin and mix well. Pour into sterilized jars and refrigerate.
   Great as an appetizer with cream cheese and crackers, or as a condiment with meat.

Yield 3½ cups

Found in the Southwest, it is quickly spreading across the country.

25-30 cucumbers, sliced
8 large onions, chopped
2 green peppers, chopped
½ c. non-iodized salt
5 c. apple cider vinegar
7 c. sugar
2 T. mustard seed
1 tsp. ground turmeric
1 tsp. ground cloves

Mix vegetables together and sprinkle with salt. Let stand for 3 hours in glass or crockery bowl. In large heavy pot or kettle, combine vinegar, sugar and seasonings; bring to a boil. Drain and rinse vegetables and drop into boiling syrup. Heat through but do not boil. Pack while hot in sterilized jars and seal tightly.

Yield 14 pints

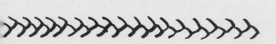

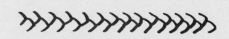

Kosher Dill Pickles

Pink Pickled Eggs

1 bushel cucumbers, small and
  medium size
4 bags ice cubes
12 whole fresh garlic bulbs
5 large bunches fresh dill, rinsed
  well and trimmed
carrot and celery sticks (optional)
40-1 qt. canning jars and caps,
  sterilized (zinc caps and rubber
  rings may be used)
pickling spice, 1 tsp. per jar
  (optional)
1 box Kosher coarse salt

Use double wash tubs or sinks. In
one tub place cucumbers in cold
water. Scrub well and place in the
other tub of cold water with the
bags of ice cubes. Let crisp while
you prepare other ingredients.

Peel and cut garlic into medium-size pieces. Cut dill into
sprigs. Cut up carrots and celery
into sticks. Line up jars and place
in each jar: 3-5 garlic pieces, cucumbers (4-5 larger cukes for the
first layer in "standing up" posi-
tion, using smaller cukes for top
layer), one large or several small
sprigs of dill, pickling spice, carrot and celery sticks.

Dissolve 1 cup of the coarse
Kosher salt in 15 cups of cold
water. Repeat as needed. Pour
into jars and fill to top, making
sure water covers all the pickles.
Cap tight and continue tightening
daily. It is normal for the pickles
to "work" in the jar which will
cause bubbling and seeping. Keep
tightening jars daily. For "half
dills", check after 4-5 days, green
color is a good indicator. To keep
them "half dill" longer, refrigerate. If possible, pickles should be
refrigerated after 8-10 days.

Yield 40 quarts

Prize winning recipe.

6 hard-cooked eggs
1 lb. fresh medium beets, cooked
  and sliced
1 c. beet juice from cooking beets
1 c. vinegar
2 T. sugar
¾ tsp. salt
½ tsp. each whole cloves and
  allspice

Peel eggs and place in deep glass
bowl, cover with sliced beets.
Combine remaining ingredients in
saucepan, heat to boiling, pour
over eggs and beets. Refrigerate
for 4 hours or overnight. Remove
eggs from beet juice and serve
whole or cut in half lengthwise.
Remove beets from juice and
serve as pickled beets. A 16 ounce
can of medium beets plus water to
make juice equal 1 cup, may be
used instead of fresh beets and
juice.

Yield 6 eggs

*Beautiful to look at and delightful to
eat. A great conversation piece to
any buffet.*

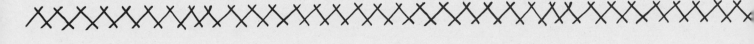

American
Powdered Sugar Frosting

American
Penuche Frosting

3 c. powdered sugar
1/3 c. soft butter
1½ tsp. vanilla or flavoring of
  your choice
2 T. milk (use more or less as
  desired)

Mix the sugar and butter together. Stir in vanilla and add milk to desired consistency.

Yield — Frosts a 2-layer cake or a 9″ x 13″ cake

Vary this with flavor and color.

1/3 c. butter
2/3 c. brown sugar
3 T. milk
1 to 1½ c. sifted powdered sugar

Melt butter in saucepan. Stir in brown sugar. Bring to a boil and cook stirring constantly over low heat for 2 minutes. Add milk, bring to a boil again and stir constantly. Remove from heat and cool to lukewarm (102 degrees). Sift in powdered sugar and beat until thick and of spreading consistency. Use on any kind of cake or brownies.

Yield 1 cup

Can add more powdered sugar and some chopped walnuts and you will have penuche fudge.

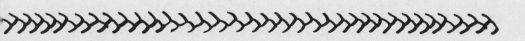

happy endings

desserts & sweets

German
Apple Bundt Cake

2 c. granulated sugar
¼ c. orange juice
1 c. vegetable oil
2½ tsp. vanilla
4 eggs
3 c. flour
3 tsp. baking powder
½ tsp. salt
1 c. chopped nuts
powdered sugar for topping

Filling:
2 c. apples, peeled and diced
1 tsp. cinnamon
1 T. sugar

Beat first five ingredients at high speed. Sift dry ingredients, then blend with first mixture. Fold in nuts. Place ⅓ of batter in a greased bundt pan. Combine filling ingredients, put some filling on top and alternate mixtures, ending with batter. Bake 55-60 minutes at 350 degrees. Remove from pan while hot. Cool cake and sprinkle with powdered sugar.

10-12 servings

American
Apple Cake

½ c. soft butter
1½ c. sugar
2 eggs
¼ c. boiling water
2 c. flour
2 tsp. baking powder
½ tsp. salt
3 apples, peeled, cored and sliced
   ½" thick
¼ c. sugar
½ tsp. cinnamon

Cream butter and 1½ cup sugar; beat in eggs. Slowly add boiling water and beat. Sift flour, baking powder and salt; stir into creamed mixture. Spread into greased 9" x 13" pan. Cover with sliced apples, arranged in rows. Combine ¼ cup sugar and cinnamon; sprinkle over apples. Bake at 350 degrees for 45 minutes.

16-20 servings

American
Molasses Cake

2 T. shortening
½ c. brown sugar
½ c. granulated sugar
2 eggs, beaten
¾ c. light molasses
1 tsp. ginger
1 tsp. cinnamon
dash of cloves
pinch of salt
2 c. flour
1 tsp. baking soda
1 c. buttermilk

Cream shortening and add sugars; blend well. Add beaten eggs and mix thoroughly. Add molasses. Sift the next five ingredients together. Mix the soda and buttermilk and add alternately with the flour mixture. Pour into greased and floured 9" x 13" pan. Bake at 350 degrees for 35-40 minutes. A powdered sugar icing flavored with orange is nice with this cake.

12-14 servings

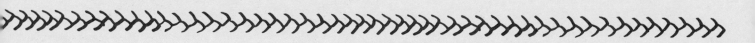

American
Cranberry Cake

1 c. sifted flour
1 tsp. baking powder
½ c. sugar
½ c. milk
1½ T. melted butter
1 c. cranberries, cut in half

Sauce:
¼ c. butter
1 c. sugar
¾ c. heavy cream
1 tsp. vanilla

Sift dry ingredients together and add the milk. Stir in melted butter and cranberries; pour into greased and floured 8" pie or cake pan. Bake at 350 degrees for 30 minutes. For sauce, brown butter lightly in a skillet and slowly add the sugar, stirring carefully. Next add the cream and vanilla and bring to a boil. Pour warm sauce over cake. Sauce can be reheated.

6 servings

A sweet and sour taste combination, great for the holidays, especially Thanksgiving.

German
Rhubarb Cake

½ c. shortening
1½ c. brown sugar
1 egg
½ tsp. salt
1 tsp. cinnamon
¼ tsp. allspice
¼ tsp. cloves
1 tsp. vanilla
2 c. finely chopped rhubarb
2 c. plus 2 T. flour
1 tsp. baking soda
1 c. buttermilk or soured milk (see substitutions)

Topping:
½ c. sugar
1 tsp. cinnamon
½ c. chopped nuts
½ c. coconut

Mix first eight ingredients well, then add rhubarb and set aside. In a separate bowl, mix flour and soda. Alternately, add flour and buttermilk to first mixture. Mix well and pour batter in a greased 9" x 13" pan. Combine topping ingredients and sprinkle on batter. Bake in a 350 degree oven for about 40 minutes.

20-24 servings

This is a moist cake and improves with age.

English
Tipsy Parson Cake

3 eggs
¼ c. sugar
1/8 tsp. salt
2 c. milk, scalded
1 angel food or layer cake
½ c. cream sherry
sweetened whipped cream

Beat eggs to blend; add sugar, salt and scalded milk. Cook in double boiler over hot but not boiling water, stirring constantly until custard coats the spoon, about 7 minutes; cool. Cut cake into 3 layers (4 for layer cake); stir sherry into custard. Place first layer of cake cut side up on plate. Pour ½ cup of custard over. Repeat with other layers, pouring last of custard over completed cake. Chill overnight. Serve with whipped cream.

12 servings

Yugoslavian
Poticia Cake

¾ c. soft butter or margarine
1½ c. granulated sugar
4 eggs
1 pt. sour cream
1 tsp. vanilla
3 c. flour
1½ tsp. baking powder
1½ tsp. baking soda
1 c. chopped nuts
1 tsp. cinnamon
1½ c. brown sugar
2 T. flour
powdered sugar

Cream butter and granulated sugar. Add eggs, one at a time. Add sour cream and vanilla. Sift 3 cups flour, baking powder and soda together three times and add to mixture, mixing well. Combine nuts, cinnamon, brown sugar and 2 tablespoons flour; fold into batter. Bake at 350 degrees for 60-65 minutes in a greased bundt pan. When cool, remove and sprinkle with powdered sugar.

12 servings

Jewish
Passover Sponge Cake

10 eggs, separated
3 T. water
1 c. sugar
¾ c. matzo cake meal
¼ c. potato starch
juice of ½ lemon

Beat egg yolks, water and sugar until lemon colored. Sift matzo cake meal and starch together; add to beaten yolks. Add lemon juice. Beat egg whites until very stiff, fold carefully into batter. Bake in ungreased 10" tube pan in 350 degree oven for 50 minutes. Invert pan to cool. May be served with strawberries and whipped cream.

16 servings

Traditional cake for Passover holiday.

American
Cheap Cake or War Cake

Eggless, Milkless, Butterless Cake

1 c. sugar
1 c. water
1 c. raisins
⅓ c. lard or vegetable shortening
1 tsp. cinnamon
½ tsp. cloves
¼ tsp. nutmeg
2 c. flour
1 tsp. baking powder
¼ tsp. salt
1 tsp. baking soda dissolved in 1 tsp. hot water

Boil the sugar, water, raisins, lard and spices together for 3 minutes. Mix flour, baking powder and salt together. When boiled mixture is cool, stir in flour mixture, blending well. Stir in the dissolved soda and pour into greased 8½" loaf pan. Bake at 350 degrees for 50-60 minutes.

Yield 1 loaf cake

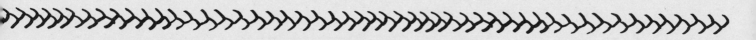

German
Sauerkraut Chocolate Cake

1½ c. sugar
⅔ c. soft margarine
3 eggs
1 tsp. vanilla
2½ c. flour
1 tsp. baking powder
1 tsp. baking soda
¼ tsp. salt
½ c. cocoa
1 c. water
⅔ c. sauerkraut, drained and
   chopped

Frosting:
¼ c. flour
1 c. milk
½ c. soft butter
½ c. shortening
1 c. powdered sugar
1 tsp. vanilla
¼ c. cocoa (optional)

In a large mixing bowl, cream sugar and margarine. Add eggs and vanilla. Sift dry ingredients together and add to creamed mixture alternating with water. Add sauerkraut and blend. Bake in greased and floured 9" x 13" pan for 35 minutes at 350 degrees or until wooden pick inserted into cake center comes out clean.

For frosting, mix flour and milk in saucepan until smooth. Cook over low heat until thick, stirring constantly. Cool thoroughly. Cream butter and shortening with electric mixer for 2 minutes; add flour-milk mixture, powdered sugar and vanilla. If desired, add cocoa. Frost cake when cool.

24 servings

The sauerkraut in this cake resembles and tastes like coconut. It will fool your cake-eaters!

Greek
Karithopeta

Walnut Cake

3 eggs
1½ c. sugar
1 c. vegetable oil
1 c. soured milk or buttermilk
2¼ c. sifted cake flour
1 T. baking powder
½ tsp. baking soda
1 tsp. cinnamon
1 tsp. cloves
1 c. chopped walnuts

Syrup:
1½ c. sugar
1 c. water
juice and rind from ½ lemon
1 stick cinnamon

Mix the first four ingredients together until well blended. Mix remaining ingredients in a bowl, then add to first mixture. Mix slowly and thoroughly, scraping sides and bottom of bowl. Bake in greased 9" x 13" pan at 350 degrees for 35-40 minutes. Cool cake thoroughly in pan. Cut into diamond shapes. Boil syrup ingredients in saucepan for 5 minutes and pour over the cooled cake.

12-14 servings

Swedish
Pecan Balls

½ c. soft butter or margarine
2 T. granulated sugar
1 c. ground pecans
1/8 tsp. salt
1 c. sifted flour
1 tsp. vanilla
1 c. powdered sugar

Cream butter and granulated sugar; add nuts, salt, flour and vanilla. Mix until well blended. Shape mixture into balls about the size of a walnut. Place on ungreased cookie sheet and bake in 375 degree oven for 12 minutes or until lightly browned. Shake in bag of powdered sugar while hot and again after cookies have cooled.

Yield 2½-3 dozen

Norwegian
Sugar Cookies

1 c. soft butter
1½ c. sugar
2 eggs, beaten
2¼ c. flour
1 tsp. cream of tartar
½ tsp. baking soda
1 tsp. vanilla

Cream butter and sugar. Add eggs and rest of ingredients. (Dough will be sticky, keep it cool.) When rolling out dough, use as little flour on the board as possible so that cookies will be rich and very crisp. Cut into various shapes with cookie cutters. Bake on lightly greased cookie sheet at 350 degrees for 12 minutes or just until the edges turn golden. Cookies may be frosted or sprinkled with pearl or granulated sugar.

Yield about 3 dozen

Pearl sugar is a larger granulated sugar and found at supermarkets and specialty stores.

Swedish
Sour Cream Sugar Cookies

2 c. sugar
1 c. shortening
2 eggs
1 c. sour cream
1 tsp. vanilla
6 c. flour
1 tsp. baking soda
½ tsp. salt

Cream sugar and shortening together. Add eggs, sour cream and vanilla. Sift flour, baking soda and salt together. Add to creamed mixture. Chill in refrigerator about 45 minutes. Roll dough ¼" thick and cut with cookie cutter. Bake on greased cookie sheet in 375 degree oven for 8-10 minutes or until golden.

Yield 6 dozen

This fourth generation cookie is nice served at Christmas decorated with colored frosting.

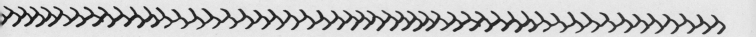

Norwegian
Brown Sugar Cookies

1 c. soft butter
2 c. brown sugar
2 eggs
2 c. flour
1 tsp. salt
1 tsp. baking soda dissolved in a
    little water
¾ c. coconut
1 c. raisins
2 c. ground oatmeal (use food
    processor, blender or grinder)

Cream butter and sugar. Add
eggs and beat well. Mix in flour,
salt and soda until well blended.
Stir in remaining ingredients and
drop by teaspoonfuls onto
ungreased cookie sheet. Bake at
350 degrees for 10-12 minutes.

Yield 5 dozen

*An old "passed down" family recipe
in which each generation adds a new
ingredient.*

German
Anise Cookies

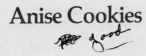
good

6 eggs, well beaten **3**
2½ c. sugar 1 ¼
3 c. flour 1 ½
1 tsp. anise flavoring ½

Beat eggs and sugar thoroughly
with an electric beater for at least
20 minutes. The top should be
covered with bubbles. Add flour
and flavoring. Drop batter from
teaspoon onto greased cookie
sheets and let stand overnight
(minimum of 8 hours). The next
morning, bake at 375 degrees
until lightly browned, about 6-8
minutes.

Yield 6 dozen

Jewish
Poppy Seed Cookies

3 eggs
1 c. sugar
¾ c. vegetable oil
1 tsp. vanilla
3 T. milk
4 c. flour
2 rounded tsp. baking powder
¼ tsp. baking soda
dash of salt
¼ c. poppy seeds
sugar for sprinkling

With a wooden spoon, cream
eggs and 1 cup sugar, gradually
add oil, vanilla and milk. Mix dry
ingredients together and gradually add to egg mixture. Add
poppy seeds. Chill and roll out
dough very thin on floured board
and cut into 2" circles. Sprinkle
with sugar and bake in a 350
degree oven for 10-12 minutes or
until golden brown.

Yield about 7-8 dozen

Often called Mohn cookies.

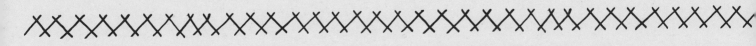

German
Oatmeal Cookies

American
Old-Fashioned Molasses Cookies

American
Ginger Creams

1 c. soft butter
¾ c. powdered sugar
1 tsp. vanilla
1¾ c. flour
½ tsp. salt
1 c. rolled oats
powdered sugar for rolling

Cream butter and ¾ cup sugar. Add vanilla. Mix in flour and salt, then oats. Shape dough into small crescents, logs or thumbprints. Bake at 300 degrees on lightly greased cookie sheet for 30 minutes. Roll in powdered sugar while cookies are still warm.

Yield 3 dozen

1½ c. sifted flour
¾ tsp. baking soda
½ tsp. salt
¼ tsp. ginger
½ tsp. cinnamon
½ c. vegetable shortening
¾ c. sugar
1 egg
¼ c. molasses
½ c. coconut
½ c. chopped walnuts

Sift flour, soda, salt, ginger and cinnamon together. Cream shortening and sugar well; blend with dry ingredients. Add egg, molasses, coconut and walnuts and mix well. Drop by rounded teaspoonfuls onto greased cookie sheet, allowing 2″ between cookies. Top with additional nuts and coconut, if desired. Bake at 350 degrees for 10 minutes. Cool slightly before removing from cookie sheets.

Yield 4-5 dozen

1 c. molasses
1¼ c. sugar
1 T. baking soda
1 c. lard or vegetable shortening
1 c. cold coffee
1 tsp. ginger
1 tsp. cinnamon
1 tsp. cloves
4½ c. flour

Mix ingredients in order listed. Dough will be so stiff a spoon in it will stand upright. Drop by teaspoonfuls onto lightly greased cookie sheet. Bake in 375 degree oven for 12 minutes. When cool, cookies may be frosted with Powdered Sugar Frosting (see index).

Yield 11 dozen cookies

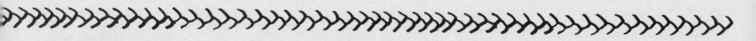

American

Gingerbread Boys or Men

1 c. vegetable shortening
1 c. light brown sugar
1 c. dark molasses
1 c. hot water
5 c. sifted flour
1 T. baking soda
½ tsp. ginger
1 tsp. salt
raisins (optional)

In a mixing bowl, combine the shortening, brown sugar, molasses and water. Sift together dry ingredients and add, mixing well. Dough will be sticky. Chill dough thoroughly and roll out on a floured board or pastry cloth ¼" thick. Cut into gingerbread boys and use raisins for decorations, if desired. Bake in a 350 degree oven for 8-10 minutes. Use colored icing for additional garnishing such as hats, hair, belts and shoes. Add water and coloring to powdered sugar and apply with a wooden pick or small spatula.

Yield 5-6 dozen

Today's definition might be "gingerbread persons." This treat is for kids the world over; fun to cut out and decorate.

Scottish

Gingersnaps

1½ c. shortening
1 c. sugar
2 eggs
½ c. light molasses
4 c. flour
2 tsp. baking soda
2 tsp. cinnamon
2 tsp. cloves
2 tsp. ginger
1 tsp. salt
granulated sugar for dipping

Cream shortening and sugar; beat in eggs and molasses. Add dry ingredients except sugar for dipping. Roll into 1" balls. Dip in sugar. Place on lightly greased cookie sheet, 2" apart. Bake in a 350 degree oven about 15 minutes. They will crack.

Yield 6 dozen

Scottish

Brandysnaps

2 T. sugar
2 T. maple syrup
2 T. butter
2 T. flour
1½ tsp. ginger

Place all ingredients in order given in a small pan and heat on stove, mixing well. Drop by tablespoonfuls on a greased cookie sheet about 2" apart. Bake 6-8 minutes or until brown in a 350 degree oven. Remove from sheet with spatula while warm and roll to form cone or cylinder. When ready to serve, fill with sweetened whipped cream or ice cream and top with fudge sauce.

Yield 4 Brandysnaps

An elegant dessert.

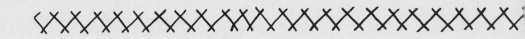

Scandinavian
Rosettes

Deep Fried Cookies

2 eggs
1 tsp. granulated sugar
¼ tsp. salt
1 c. milk
¼ c. cornstarch
¾ c. flour
lard or peanut oil for frying
powdered sugar

Beat eggs lightly. Add granulated sugar, salt and milk. Mix in cornstarch sifted with flour. Heat rosette iron in deep fat (375-400 degrees). Keep a thick cloth spread by the pan to tap iron for removing excess fat. Dip iron carefully in the thin batter and fry. Remove the rosette by tapping iron lightly with a fork. Dust with powdered sugar.

Yield 4½ dozen

These can be made in timbale forms and filled with creamed seafoods or chicken ala king as main dishes for luncheons, without the powdered sugar.

Norwegian
Krumkake

Thin Cone-Shaped Cookies

½ c. whipping cream
3 eggs
1 c. sugar
½ c. melted butter
1¼ c. flour
1 tsp. ground cardamom or 1 tsp.
   almond extract

Whip the cream. Beat eggs lightly and add to the cream. Add remaining ingredients. Bake on a krumkake iron on top of the stove. Turn the iron once while baking each cookie. Remove krumkake from the iron with a spatula. Roll at once around a wooden krumkake roller; cool and remove.

Yield 6 dozen 5" cookies

Try filling with sweetened whipped cream and strawberry preserves.

Scandinavian
Krumkake

Thin Cone-Shaped Cookies

½ c. sugar
1 c. whipping cream
1 c. flour
pinch of salt
½-1 tsp. vanilla

Stir sugar into cream. Add flour and salt; beat until smooth. Add vanilla. Drop by teaspoonfuls onto a hot krumkake iron. Turn to brown both sides, remove and quickly roll into a cone.

Yield 5 dozen

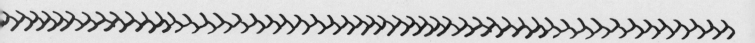

Finnish
Suomalaiset Puikot

Cookie Sticks

1 c. soft butter
½ c. sugar
1 egg
1 tsp. almond extract
¼ tsp. salt
3 c. sifted flour
3 eggs, beaten
sugar for coating
1½ c. finely chopped almonds

Cream butter and ½ cup sugar until well mixed; add egg, almond extract and salt. Add flour, working with hands until it forms a smooth dough, and shape into long rolls about ¾" thick. Cut into 3" lengths and dip in eggs, then sugar, then almonds. Place in rows on greased cookie sheets. Bake at 350 degrees for 8-10 minutes or until very lightly browned.

Yield 5 dozen

An old Finnish tradition well worth the time spent.

Jewish
Mondelbrot

Sweet Almond Slice

½ c. soft butter
1 c. sugar
½ tsp. vanilla
½ tsp. salt
½ tsp. baking powder
2 eggs, lightly beaten
2⅓ c. flour
⅓-½ c. blanched, chopped almonds

Cream butter and sugar together; add vanilla, salt and baking powder and mix thoroughly. Add eggs and flour, a little at a time. Knead until smooth. Add almonds and knead again until they are evenly distributed.

With greased hands, divide dough into 2 parts. Place each part on greased cookie sheet; pat dough into two rectangles the length of the cookie sheet 1½" x 2" wide by ½" thick. Bake at 350 degrees for 25-30 minutes. While still warm, cut with a greased knife into ½" slices. Place on cookie sheet and bake another 10 minutes until brown.

Yield 4 dozen ½" slices

Italian
Italian Cookie Toast

1 c. soft butter or margarine
1 c. sugar
2 eggs
1 tsp. baking soda
1 tsp. baking powder
¼ tsp. cardamom
3½ c. flour
1 c. sour cream

Cream butter and sugar. Add eggs and beat well. Mix dry ingredients and add alternately with sour cream. Bake in 2 greased bread pans. If smaller pans are used, use 4 pans. Bake at 350 degrees for 45 minutes. Slice while still warm, then place on cookie sheets to brown in a 300 degree oven a few minutes longer. Store in tight container and these will keep for months.

Yield 2-4 loaves

Serve with a glass of wine.

Plain Kamish Bread

A Cookie

4 eggs
1 c. sugar
1 c. vegetable oil
3½ c. flour
1 tsp. baking powder
pinch of salt
1 tsp. cinnamon
1 (4 oz.) pkg. sliced almonds

Mix eggs and sugar, gradually beat in oil. Sift dry ingredients and add almonds. Combine with egg mixture. Roll into 4 rolls on a well-floured board. Place rolls side by side in a greased 9" x 13" pan. Bake at 350 degrees for 30 minutes.

When bread is slightly cooled, slice in ¾" pieces and put on a large cookie sheet. Bake in a 300 degree oven about 10 minutes on each side until golden brown.

Yield 32-36 pieces

A toasted cookie.

Chocolate Fudge Kamish Bread

A Rich Cookie

1¼ c. soft butter
1 c. brown sugar
3 c. flour
1 tsp. salt
1 T. milk
1 tsp. vanilla
1 (12 oz.) pkg. semisweet chocolate chips
1 can sweetened condensed milk
1 T. butter
1 c. chopped walnuts

Cream butter and brown sugar. Mix with flour, salt, milk and vanilla and divide dough into 4 parts. Melt chocolate chips, condensed milk and butter in double boiler. Roll out each part on floured waxed paper. Spread each with ¼ of chocolate mixture and sprinkle with ¼ cup nuts. Roll up, using waxed paper as a guide. Bake for 25 minutes at 350 degrees on greased cookie sheet, 4" apart as they spread while baking. Cool in the pans and then cut into slices.

Yield 4 small rolls; 48 pieces

For experienced pastry bakers . . .

Shortbread

1 lb. soft butter
1 c. sugar
⅔ c. rice flour
4 c. white flour
granulated sugar

Cream butter and 1 cup sugar well (may use hands). Add flours gradually and divide into 3 parts. Pat out into three lightly greased 8" square pans. Prick all over with fork and bake at 300 degrees for about 30 minutes or until light brown. Sprinkle with sugar and cut into 1" squares while warm.

Yield 16 dozen

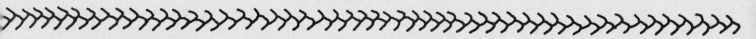

Czechoslovakian
Bohemian Nut Slices

1 pkg. dry yeast
¼ c. warm water
1 tsp. granulated sugar
2 c. sifted flour
½ tsp. salt
¾ c. butter or margarine
2 eggs, separated
½ c. granulated sugar
1 tsp. vanilla
¼ c. chopped nuts
powdered sugar

Sprinkle yeast over warm water. Add 1 teaspoon granulated sugar and let stand 10 minutes or until yeast is softened. Sift together flour and salt. Cut in butter until mixture resembles coarse meal.

Blend in egg yolks and yeast. Mix until a smooth ball is formed. Beat egg whites until stiff but not dry. Gradually beat in ½ cup granulated sugar. Continue beating until stiff peaks form. Fold in vanilla.

Divide dough in half. Roll out each half on lightly floured surface into a 9" x 13" rectangle. Spread with egg white mixture and sprinkle with nuts. Roll up as for a jelly roll, starting at long side. Place rolls on greased cookie sheet. Make ½" deep cut down center of each roll lengthwise. Bake at 375 degrees for 22 minutes. When still warm, sprinkle with powdered sugar. Cool thoroughly. Slice diagonally.

Yield 3½-4 dozen ½" slices

Norwegian
Chocolate Wafers

⅓ c. soft butter
2 hard-cooked egg yolks, sieved
¼ c. sugar
1 tsp. vanilla
1 c. sifted flour
½ c. semisweet chocolate chips, ground

Combine first four ingredients; blend well. Add remaining ingredients and mix. Roll between 2 sheets of waxed paper to ¼" thickness. Cut into 2" circles and bake on greased cookie sheet for 8 minutes in a 400 degree oven.

Yield 2 dozen

German

Raisin Fritters

2 c. flour
2 tsp. baking powder
2 T. granulated sugar (heaping)
2 eggs
dash of salt
1 c. milk
1 c. raisins
fat for deep frying
powdered sugar (optional)

Sift together flour, baking powder and granulated sugar. Mix eggs, salt and milk. Add liquid mixture to dry ingredients. Add raisins. Drop by spoon into hot deep fat (375 degrees). Fry until golden brown. Drain on paper towels or rack. Fritters may be sprinkled with powdered sugar, if desired.

Yield 2 dozen

Dutch

Appelbeignets

Apple Fritters

12 apples, peeled and cored
2 c. flour
1½ c. beer
½ tsp. salt
vegetable oil for frying
powdered sugar

Cut apples crosswise into ⅓″ slices. To make the fritter batter, combine flour, beer and salt. Stir with a wooden spoon until there are no more lumps in the mixture. Dip the apple slices in the batter and deep fry in hot oil. Drain fritters on paper towels and sprinkle with powdered sugar.

Yield 5 dozen

German

Apple Crisp

8 c. peeled and sliced apples
2 c. granulated sugar
¼ c. flour
1 c. brown sugar
1 c. oatmeal
1 c. flour
1 c. melted butter

Mix apples with granulated sugar and ¼ cup flour; spread in 9″ x 13″ cake pan. Blend brown sugar, oatmeal, 1 cup flour and melted butter until crumbly. Sprinkle over apples. Bake at 350 degrees for 45 minutes or until a deep golden brown. May be served with whipped cream or ice cream.

12-18 servings

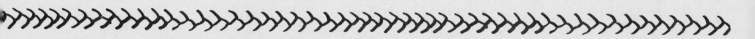

English
English Trifle

3-4 firm bananas, peeled and
  sliced
1 pt. raspberries
1 pt. strawberries
1 pt. blueberries
1 (3¾ oz.) pkg. pecans, chopped
1 (3¾ oz.) pkg. vanilla pudding
1 sponge or pound cake, sliced
1½ oz. brandy
1 pt. whipped cream mixed with 1
  tsp. brandy

Mix together all fruits with the
nuts. Prepare vanilla pudding as
directed on package. Arrange a
layer of sponge cake slices in a
large glass bowl and top with a
layer of the fruit and nut mixture
and a sprinkle of brandy. Continue in layers until about 2" from
top of bowl. Spread vanilla pudding over trifle and mound with
whipped cream.

  Place in refrigerator for 1 hour
or more, allowing flavors to min-
gle. To serve, spoon down
through trifle so that each serving
consists of whipped cream, pudding, fruit and cake.

6-8 servings

*Part of the pleasure of this dessert is
the way it looks in a glass bowl
before serving . . .*

Greek
Baklava

1 lb. phyllo (filo) leaves
¼ lb. melted butter
1 lb. unblanched almonds,
  coarsely ground
1 lb. chopped pecans
¾ c. sugar
1 tsp. ground cloves
1 tsp. cinnamon
½ tsp. allspice (optional)
36 whole cloves

Syrup:
3 c. sugar
1½ c. water
½ c. honey
juice and rind from ½ lemon
1 stick cinnamon

Butter sides and bottom of a jelly
roll pan. Place 5 or 6 phyllo
leaves in bottom, brushing each
leaf with melted butter. Combine
nuts, sugar and spices except
whole cloves and sprinkle a layer
over the leaves. Cover with 2
leaves, again buttering each layer
and sprinkling with nut and spice
mixture. Continue with layering
until all nut mixture is used,
reserving 5 or 6 leaves for the top
layer.

  Cut into 36 diamond-shaped
pieces in pan and press a whole
clove into the center of each diamond. Bake at 250 degrees for 2½
hours.

  Boil all syrup ingredients
together for 10-15 minutes. Let
cool to lukewarm. Remove cinnamon stick. Recut pastry after baking, and place cookie sheet with
sides under the baking pan and
pour lukewarm syrup over the
hot baklava. Cover with foil and
let stand about 12 hours or more.
These will keep in the refrigerator
for a week and also freeze well.

Yield 3 dozen pieces

*See recipe for Feta Cheese Pie for
additional phyllo facts.*

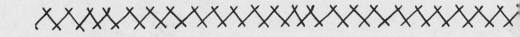

German
Black Forest Apple Strudel

4-6 apples, peeled and sliced
2 T. cinnamon
½ c. raisins
½ c. sliced almonds
2 c. sugar
juice from 1 lemon
½ c. bread crumbs
½ pkg. strudel dough (phyllo or filo leaves)
½ c. melted butter
cinnamon-sugar (optional)

Mix apples, cinnamon, raisins and almonds with 1¾ cups sugar and lemon juice. Add remaining ¼ cup sugar to bread crumbs in separate bowl. Have a large clean cloth covering table, sprinkle lightly with water. Work fast and carefully. Lay one sheet of dough on cloth and brush with butter.

Sprinkle with ¼ of the sugar-bread crumb mixture. Repeat this, layering 3 more sheets on top of first (4 layers in all). Now spread apple mixture in a line along with the dough, leaving a 2" border on the bottom and a 1" border on each side. Roll into a tight loaf by pulling up and forward on the bottom edge of cloth. Fold dough in at borders and seal all edges with butter.

Carefully place loaf in buttered sheet pan with sides to catch juices. Brush with melted butter. Sprinkle the top of loaf with cinnamon-sugar. Bake in 375 degree oven for 45 minutes or until well browned. Serve hot or cold with whipped cream or ice cream.

Yield 1 large loaf

Czechoslovakian
Cottage Cheese Squares

Fruit Filled Pastry

1 c. soft butter
1 c. cottage cheese (fairly dry)
2 c. sifted flour
pinch of salt
1½ c. thick apple butter, apricot filling or jam of choice
powdered sugar

Cream butter and cottage cheese together. Cut and work in the flour and salt; then work with hands to form a dough. Wrap in heavy waxed paper and chill well in refrigerator. When cold, roll out slightly thicker than for pie crust and cut into 2" squares. Use a sharp knife to cut. Place a teaspoonful of filling in the center of each square. Fold corners toward middle to form a pocket. Place on greased cookie sheet and bake in 425 degree oven about 15 minutes or until puffed and lightly browned. Sprinkle with powdered sugar and cool.

Yield 4 dozen cookies

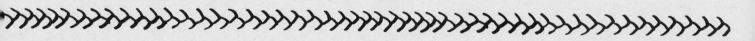

American
Filled Cookies

1 egg
1 c. sugar
½ c. lard or soft butter
½ c. soured milk
1 tsp. baking soda
1 tsp. vanilla
2 tsp. cream of tartar
2¼ c. flour

Filling:
2 c. pitted dates or raisins, ground
½ c. sugar
1 T. flour
½ c. water
1 tsp. soft butter
½ tsp. vanilla

Mix dough ingredients in order given. Roll out 1/8″ thin and cut in 2″ rounds. Mix filling ingredients together and place teaspoonful a little off center on each round. Fold dough over filling and press edges. Bake on lightly greased cookie sheets at 350 degrees for 10-12 minutes. Can also be made as plain sugar cookies.

Yield 5 dozen

This recipe dates back to 1876 and passed down in one family for over 100 years.

Jewish
Hamantashen

Fruit Filled Holiday Cookie

4 eggs
3 c. sugar
9 c. flour
2 tsp. baking powder
2 tsp. baking soda
1½ c. vegetable shortening
1½ c. sour cream
juice and grated rind of 2 oranges
grated rind of 2 lemons
1 beaten egg, thinned with water

Filling:
1 lb. dried pitted apricots
½ lb. dried pitted prunes
½ lb. seedless golden raisins
water for boiling
2 T. orange juice and grated rind
  to taste
2 T. lemon juice and grated rind
  to taste
1 T. sugar to taste
plum jam (optional)
coconut (optional)
chopped nuts (optional)

Beat 4 eggs and sugar. Sift flour, baking powder and baking soda together and add to eggs. Cut in shortening. Add sour cream and juice and grated rinds; mix thoroughly. Cover bowl and refrigerate overnight.

In large saucepan, cover dried fruit with water and bring to a boil. Remove from heat and let fruit soak until soft, about 30-45 minutes. Drain fruits well; grind together and add orange and lemon juice, rind and sugar to taste. Can also mix in any of the optional ingredients.

On a lightly floured board, roll out dough about 1/8″ thick. Cut dough into 3″ rounds, using cookie cutter. Place a heaping teaspoonful of filling on each round. Fold 3 sides together to meet over filling, pinch together to make a three-cornered cookie. Brush with beaten egg thinned with water. Bake on ungreased cookie sheet at 350 degrees about 10-15 minutes or until golden.

Yield about 8 dozen

A specialty during the Holiday of Purim.

German
Peppernuts

Hard Cookies

2 c. sifted flour
¾ tsp. cardamom
¾ tsp. baking powder
¾ tsp. allspice
¾ tsp. salt
¾ tsp. mace
¾ tsp. baking soda
¼ tsp. black pepper
¼ tsp. ground anise seed
1 c. honey
3 T. shortening
1 egg

Sift dry ingredients. Heat the honey, but do not boil; add shortening; cool. Beat in the egg; stir in dry ingredients just until blended. Let dough stand 10 minutes to stiffen enough to handle. Shape into 1½" balls. Place on greased cookie sheet. Bake at 350 degrees 12-13 minutes. Cool cookies, then frost with Powdered Sugar Frosting (see index). Store in airtight container to ripen.

Yield 3 dozen

Often referred to as Pfeffernusse.

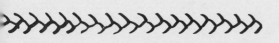

Welsh
Welsh Cakes

Sweet Fried Cakes

4 c. flour
1 tsp. salt
4 tsp. baking powder
1½ c. sugar
1 c. currants, steamed
¼ c. butter
¾ c. vegetable shortening
3 eggs and milk to make 1 c.
1 tsp. vanilla
shortening for frying

Mix first five ingredients. Add butter and shortening and cut into flour as for a pie crust. Beat the eggs and put into a measuring cup with enough milk to total 1 cup. Add vanilla. Combine egg and milk with the flour mixture. Using a pastry cloth and rolling pin, flatten dough to about ¼" thickness. Cut into 2" diameter circles with a cookie cutter or glass. Preheat electric frypan to 325 degrees. Add a small amount of shortening and fry 6-7 minutes on each side. Add more shortening as needed.

Yield about 6 dozen

These cakes were served all year long, but especially on St. David's Day.

German
Springerle

Cookies with a Design

4 large eggs, well beaten
2 c. sugar
2 T. melted butter
3 T. sweet cream
3¾ c. flour
1 T. baking powder
1½ tsp. anise flavoring

Combine beaten eggs and sugar; mix well. Add butter, cream, flour, baking powder and flavoring. Roll to ¼" thickness. Using a springerle rolling pin, roll on pattern. Cut apart and let stand overnight to dry top. Bake on lightly greased cookie sheets at 325 degrees for 13-15 minutes.

Yield 5-6 dozen

Springerle means "little horse" and the original cookies were in the shapes of horses.

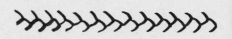

German
Lebkuchen

Honey Bars

¾ c. unblanched almonds
2 oz. (½ c.) candied orange peel
2 oz. (½ c.) candied lemon peel
3 c. sifted flour
¼ tsp. baking soda
1 tsp. cinnamon
½ tsp. allspice
½ tsp. nutmeg
½ tsp. cloves
2 eggs
1 c. granulated sugar
½ c. honey
⅓ c. sifted powdered sugar
1 T. water
1 tsp. lemon juice

Finely chop almonds, orange and lemon peel; set aside. Sift flour, baking soda and spices together; set aside. Beat eggs and granulated sugar together until thick and fluffy. Beat in honey. Gently fold in dry ingredients in fourths. Mix in almonds and candied peel. Turn batter into 10" x 15" jelly roll pan, spreading to corners. Bake at 350 degrees for 25-30 minutes or until a wooden pick comes out clean; cool. Meanwhile, blend powdered sugar, water and lemon juice. Spread evenly over top of cooled bars and cut into 3" x 1½" pieces. Store in a tightly covered jar or tin and they will keep up to six months.

Yield 2½ dozen bars

Jewish
Kichel

Dry Airy Cookies

3 eggs
pinch of salt
1 T. sugar
¾ c. vegetable oil
1 c. flour
granulated sugar for topping

Beat eggs with salt; add 3 teaspoons sugar and oil and beat thoroughly. Add flour gradually and beat for 10 minutes, pushing dough down in bowl. Lightly grease a cookie sheet and drop dough by teaspoonfuls 1" apart. Sprinkle with sugar. Bake in 375 degree oven for 10 minutes; 350 degree oven for 10 minutes more and 325 degree oven for another 25-30 minutes.

Yield 2 dozen

These are good served with sweet red wine on holidays and special occasions.

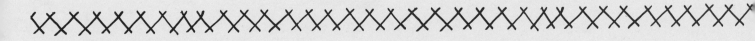

Dutch
Sneeuwballen

Snowballs

½ c. cold water
¼ tsp. salt
½ c. butter
10 T. (scant ¾ c.) sifted flour
3 large eggs
2 T. currants or raisins
2 T. finely cut citron
1 T. rum
vegetable oil or fat for frying
powdered sugar

Place water, salt and butter in saucepan and bring to boil. Remove from heat and add flour all at once. Stir with wooden spoon until smooth. Add eggs, one at a time, beating well after each addition. Add currants, citron and rum. Heat oil to 360-375 degrees. With a metal tablespoon (which should be dipped in hot oil first), cut off a spoonful of batter and fry until golden brown on both sides. These will puff up and become very light. Drain on brown paper or paper towels and sprinkle with powdered sugar to give the appearance of snow.

Yield 24 balls

A good New Year's Eve treat.

German
Munchen

Almond Cookies

1 c. soft butter
1 c. granulated sugar
½ lb. almonds, finely ground
1 tsp. vanilla
2 c. sifted flour (scant)
powdered sugar

Cream butter; then mixing by hand, add granulated sugar, almonds, vanilla and flour. Roll into 1″ balls and bake on lightly greased cookie sheet at 300 degrees until slightly brown, about 45 minutes. Let cool and dust twice with powdered sugar.

Yield 5 dozen

Chinese
Almond Cookies

1 c. lard
1 egg
1 c. sugar
2 c. flour
½ tsp. baking soda
5 drops yellow food coloring
1 tsp. almond extract
1 egg, beaten
60 whole blanched almonds

Mix first seven ingredients in bowl. Form into one or two rolls, 1″ in diameter. Cut into sixty ½″ pieces. Place on lightly greased cookie sheet ¾″ apart. Brush with beaten egg. Press 1 whole almond in center of each cookie. Bake at 375 degrees for 15 minutes.

Yield 5 dozen

A nice ending to a Chinese meal to serve along with fortune cookies and fruit.

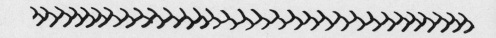

Norwegian
Fattigmand

Diamond Shaped Fried Cookies

2 eggs
4 egg yolks
6 T. granulated sugar
6 T. cream
1/8 tsp. salt
1/8 tsp. ground cardamom seed
2 T. bourbon, brandy or vanilla
2 c. flour (enough to make a soft dough)
1½ lb. lard or vegetable shortening for frying
powdered sugar (optional)

Beat eggs and egg yolks well; add granulated sugar, cream, salt and flavorings. Mix in flour to rolling consistency; chill. Roll as thin as possible and cut into diamond shapes with a pastry wheel. Drop into hot fat (370 degrees) and turn to cook both sides until lightly browned. Remove from fat and drain on paper towels. When cool, sprinkle with powdered sugar, if desired.

Yield 4 dozen

This is often called the "Poor Man" cookie.

Italian
Pizzelles

Stamped-Design Cookies

1½ c. soft margarine
1½ c. sugar
6 eggs
2 tsp. anise seed
4 tsp. baking powder
1 tsp. salt
5 c. flour

First, beg, borrow, steal or buy a pizzelle iron. Next, cream margarine and sugar together; add eggs. Add remaining ingredients and mix to form a soft cookie dough. Roll dough into small balls and bake in hot pizzelle iron for 1 minute or as directed on iron.

For pizzelles with nuts, add 1 cup of finely chopped pecans or walnuts to dough. To make Christmas pizzelles, add a few drops of red or green coloring to the dough before baking.

Yield 5 dozen

Cookies baked in a special iron on top of the stove. Store in a covered container, but do not freeze.

German
Berlinerkranze

Holiday Cookies

4 hard-cooked egg yolks, mashed
4 uncooked egg yolks
1 c. soft butter
1 c. sugar
2 c. flour
1 egg white, beaten
½ c. granulated or pearl sugar

Mix hard-cooked and uncooked egg yolks until smooth. Cream butter and 1 cup sugar; add egg yolks and beat thoroughly. Add flour. Roll into 3" strips and shape into a bow or wreath. Dip cookie in beaten egg white and then into sugar. Bake on greased cookie sheet at 300 degrees for ½ hour. Do not brown.

Yield 4 dozen

This recipe is over 100 years old.

Hungarian
Hazelnut Torte

Swiss
Apple Torte

½ lb. hazelnuts
6 eggs, separated
1-1/8 c. sugar
grated rind of 1 orange

Frosting:
½ pkg. vanilla pudding mix (not
  instant)
2 T. milk
¾ c. strong boiling coffee (2 T.
  instant dissolved in ¾ c. water)
¾ c. soft unsalted butter
¼ c. powdered sugar

Toast hazelnuts in a 350 degree oven for 15 minutes. When cool, rub with hands to remove most of the skins; then grind. Reserve 2 tablespoons for decoration. Beat egg whites until stiff. Add ½ of the sugar, then add the egg yolks, one by one. Add remaining sugar and beat well. Combine hazelnuts with orange rind, add to batter and mix well. Spread in greased 9" x 13" pan which is lined with greased waxed paper. Bake at 350 degrees for 35-40 minutes. Torte should be dark brown. Remove from pan immediately, take off waxed paper and cool.

For frosting, mix ½ package pudding with milk in a saucepan. Add boiling coffee, let come to boil and remove from heat. Cool, stirring occasionally. With mixer, cream butter and add powdered sugar. When pudding reaches room temperature, add to butter mixture by spoonfuls. Cut cake lengthwise in half and frost one half. Put other half on top and frost whole torte. Sprinkle with reserved hazelnuts.

12-16 servings

3 c. peeled and sliced apples
juice of 1 lemon
2 c. flour
2 c. sugar
1 tsp. baking powder
½ tsp. salt
¾ c. melted butter (scant)
3 eggs, separated
cinnamon-sugar (¼ c. sugar
  mixed with ½ tsp. cinnamon)

Place apples in greased 9" x 13" glass pan. Drizzle with lemon juice. Sift together flour, sugar, baking powder and salt. Sprinkle over apples. Drizzle with melted butter. Beat egg whites until stiff. Beat yolks and fold into whites and pour on top. Cover with cinnamon-sugar mixture. Bake at 325 degrees for 1 hour or until lightly browned at the edges.

12 servings

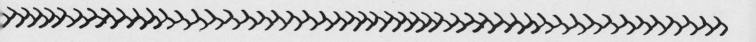

Austrian

Linzertorte

A Filled Tart

1½ c. flour
1/8 tsp. ground cloves
¼ tsp. cinnamon
1 c. finely ground unblanched
    almonds
½ c. granulated sugar
1 tsp. grated lemon rind
2 hard-cooked egg yolks, mashed
1 c. soft unsalted butter
2 uncooked egg yolks, lightly
    beaten
1 tsp. vanilla
1½ c. raspberry jam
2 T. milk
1 egg, lightly beaten
powdered sugar

Sift flour, cloves and cinnamon together. Add almonds, granulated sugar, lemon rind and mashed hard-cooked egg yolks. Beat in butter, uncooked egg yolks and vanilla until a soft dough is formed. Form into a ball, wrap in waxed paper and refrigerate for 1 hour.

Remove ¾ of dough and return ¼ to refrigerator. Lightly butter 9" loose bottom flan pan; press dough with fingers to cover bottom and sides of pan ¼" thick. Spoon on raspberry jam and spread evenly over bottom.

Roll out rest of dough into 6" x 9" rectangle ¼" thick. Cut in 1" strips, two of 9" length and the rest in 8" lengths. Lay one 9" strip across center of jam-covered shell. Place two 8" strips on each side. Rotate pan ¼ way to your left and repeat the pattern with other 3 strips so they create X's in a latticed effect.

Add milk to beaten egg and mix lightly. Brush over exposed pastry. Refrigerate ½ hour. Bake in oven on middle shelf at 350 degrees for 45-50 minutes. Cool; sprinkle with powdered sugar and serve when cool.

8-10 servings

Tastes even better the second day.

Swedish

Mazariner

Almond Tarts

1 c. soft butter
½ c. sugar
1 egg
1 tsp. vanilla
2 c. sifted flour
¼ tsp. salt

Filling:
2 eggs, well beaten
1½ c. ground blanched almonds
¼ tsp. salt
½ c. sugar
½ tsp. almond extract

Mix all crust ingredients in order given and chill 1 hour. Put about 1 teaspoonful of the mixture into each tiny greased scalloped tart pan. Press dough into sides of pan, leaving center hollow.

Combine the filling ingredients and put about 1-1½ teaspoonfuls of the mixture into each tart. Bake at 325 degrees about 25 minutes. Frost with Powdered Sugar Frosting (see index).

Yield 48 small tarts

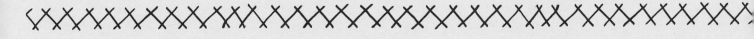

Icelandic
Vinarterta

Prune Torte with Wine

½ c. soft butter
1 c. sugar
¼ c. cream
2 eggs
½ tsp. vanilla
3 c. flour
½ tsp. baking soda
½ tsp. baking powder
1 tsp. cardamom

Filling:
1 lb. prunes
¾ c. sugar
¼ c. brandy, wine, rum or
   almond extract

Frosting:
1 c. powdered sugar
1 T. melted butter
½ T. cream
¼ tsp. brandy, wine, rum or
   almond extract

Cream butter and sugar; add cream, eggs and vanilla. Mix thoroughly but do not overbeat. Add flour, soda, baking powder and cardamom to make a soft dough. Turn out on floured surface and knead lightly. Divide dough into 5 parts; pat each part into a separate greased layer cake pan (with loose bottom preferably). Bake at 350 degrees for 15 minutes; cool. (The 5 layers will be crisp like a cookie before they soften with the filling.)

Prepare filling by removing pits from prunes and simmering in water until soft. Put through a food mill or grinder or mash through a colander. Mix well with sugar and cook until spreadable consistency. Add brandy; cool.

To assemble torte, spread about 4 tablespoons filling over each of 4 layers, arranging one on top of the other. Combine frosting ingredients, mix well and spread over top. When frosting is firm, wrap the torte in foil and let stand at room temperature for 3 days. It then may be refrigerated or frozen. To serve, cut in slices or strips across the torte and pass whipped cream or brandy for topping.

Yield one 5-layer torte

This is a traditional Icelandic Christmas treat.

Norwegian
Sandkakker

Sand Tarts

1 c. soft butter
2 c. powdered sugar
2 c. flour
4 oz. (½ c.) ground almonds

Mix ingredients together. Press very thinly into each well-buttered sandkakker pan. Bake at 375 degrees until light golden brown, about 10 minutes. Tap out of pans while still warm.

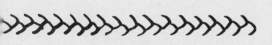

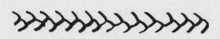

Norwegian
Sandbakkels

Sand Tarts

1 c. soft butter
1 c. sugar
1 egg
1 tsp. almond extract
2½ c. flour

Cream butter and sugar; add egg and almond extract. Add flour to make stiff dough. Press as thin as possible into well-buttered sandbakkel tins. Bake at 350 degrees for 15 minutes or until light brown. Tap out when slightly cooled.

Yield 3½ dozen

Almond flavored shells made in fluted pans.

German
Apple Tart

½ c. soft butter
1 egg yolk
¼ c. granulated sugar
1 c. flour
dash salt
½ tsp. baking powder

Apple Filling:
5-6 apples (McIntosh or Delicious)
2-3 T. lemon juice
¼ c. granulated sugar
¼ c. chopped walnuts
¼ c. raisins

Crumb Topping:
1 c. flour
1 c. brown sugar
½ c. soft butter
1 tsp. cinnamon

powdered sugar for topping
whipped cream (optional)

To make pastry shell, combine ½ cup butter, egg yolk, ¼ cup granulated sugar and beat until smooth. Stir in 1 cup flour, salt and baking powder; mix thoroughly. Wrap dough in waxed paper; chill several hours. Grease and flour 9" springform pan. Allow dough to soften slightly and press evenly over bottom and ½" up sides of pan. Bake at 375 degrees for 25-30 minutes.

Peel, core and cut apples into quarters. Slash top of each slice with a knife. Place apple slices, slashed side up, in baked pastry shell. Sprinkle with lemon juice, ¼ cup granulated sugar, walnuts and raisins. Combine topping ingredients, sprinkle over filling. Bake at 375 degrees 50-60 minutes, until lightly browned. Cool; sprinkle with powdered sugar. Serve topped with whipped cream, if desired.

8-10 servings

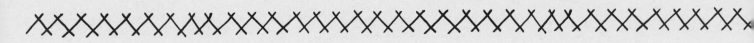

Russian
Vareniki

Dessert Dumplings

4-5 c. sifted flour, depending on
    size of eggs
3 eggs
1 tsp. salt
½ c. water

Filling:
3 c. pitted cherries, chopped
½ c. sugar
2 T. flour

1 qt. water for boiling
1 tsp. salt
¼ c. melted butter
sour cream (optional)
sugar (optional)

Put flour into large mixing bowl,
scoop out a deep hollow in the
flour and put eggs, 1 tsp. salt and
water in center. Slowly combine
and knead to make a stiff dough.
If too crumbly, add a bit more
water. Let dough stand for 45
minutes. Form 2 logs about 2" in
diameter. Slice logs into ½" circles and roll out into ½" thick
rounds.

Mix three filling ingredients
together and place a spoonful on
one half of each circle and fold
over to form a half circle. Pinch
edges together to seal. Drop Vareniki into boiling salted water and
simmer uncovered for 8-10 minutes or until they rise to the surface. Remove, drain and place on
shallow platter. Pour melted butter on top and serve hot. Top
with sour cream and sugar, if
desired.

Yield about 3 dozen

American
Maple Mousse

1 c. maple syrup
4 eggs, separated
2 c. heavy cream, whipped

In a double boiler, combine maple
syrup and egg yolks. Cook over
simmering water for 10 minutes,
stirring constantly until thickened. Remove from heat and
cool. Beat egg whites until stiff
but not dry. Fold in the whipped
cream. Beat the cooled custard
until it is light, then add it to the
egg white mixture. Spoon into a
6-cup mold and freeze until firm.

6 servings

*An excellent way to use our pure
Minnesota maple syrup tapped right
from the tree . . .*

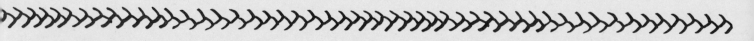

Icelandic

Orange Fromage

10 eggs, separated
¾ c. sugar
juice of 6 oranges
juice of 2 lemons
3 envelopes unflavored gelatin
1¼ c. cold water
3 c. whipping cream
1 c. whipping cream
orange slices or mandarin orange
    sections

Beat egg whites until stiff but not dry. Beat egg yolks and sugar until thick and creamy; add orange and lemon juices. In top of double boiler, sprinkle gelatin over cold water, cook over hot water and stir constantly until dissolved. Pour very slowly into egg yolk mixture, stirring constantly. Cool until mixture begins to stiffen. Beat 3 cups whipping cream until stiff. Fold beaten egg whites and whipped cream into cooled mixture. Stir gently and pour into large glass bowl; refrigerate. This can be made 2-3 days ahead. Before serving, beat 1 cup whipping cream until stiff; garnish dessert with whipped cream and thin orange slices.

20 servings

Norwegian

Römmegröt

Cream Porridge

2 pt. whipping cream
1 c. flour
1 qt. hot milk (enough for desired
    thickness)
½ tsp. salt
1 tsp. cinnamon
½ c. sugar

Simmer cream about 15 minutes, stirring occasionally. Sift in flour, stirring with whisk. Continue cooking until butterfat floats out of mixture. Pour butterfat into dish and save. Gradually add the hot milk and salt. Stir briskly with whisk until pudding is smooth.

Pour pudding into bowls. Float some of the reserved butterfat on top, and sprinkle with a mixture made from the cinnamon and sugar.

6 servings

Originating in the Dark Ages this has been considered the National Cream Porridge served on Feast Days. Tradition states that a bride should make it for her groom on their wedding day. (Definitely from the Dark Ages!)

Finnish

Vahto Puuroa

Cranberry Pudding

4 c. water
1 c. cranberries
1 c. sugar
½ c. farina
cream or half-and-half

Boil water and cranberries for 20 minutes. Strain and add sugar. Bring to a boil and add farina. Cook 15 minutes. Cool slightly. Whip until light in color and fluffy; refrigerate. Serve with cream.

6-8 servings

In Finland, the bowl was put in the snow and the pudding was whipped.

Belgian
Vlan

Belgian Pudding

11 oz. graham crackers
2 qt. cold milk
½ c. granulated sugar
2 c. brown sugar
¾ c. dark corn syrup
1 c. raisins
1 c. milk
½ c. flour
6 eggs, beaten

In a large kettle, soak the graham crackers in the 2 quarts cold milk for 10 minutes. Add both sugars, corn syrup and raisins. Bring to a boil over medium heat and cook until the mixture is well blended, stirring constantly. Remove from heat. Put 1 cup milk and flour in a pint jar, cover and shake well.

Pour this into a bowl and add some of the hot graham mixture to blend. Pour contents of bowl slowly into first mixture and stir well to prevent curdling. Cook until mixture boils. Remove from heat and add beaten eggs slowly to kettle mixture. Return to heat and cook one minute. Pour into well-buttered 4-quart crockery bowl (not glass or metal) and let stand until steam disappears. Bake in 350 degree oven for 1 hour. Cool completely. Unmold, slice and serve after it is chilled. Keeps well in refrigerator.

16-24 servings

A festive dessert especially for New Year's Day.

Swedish
Rice Pudding

2 sticks cinnamon
6 whole cloves
4 c. milk
½ c. uncooked regular rice
½ tsp. salt
1 c. sugar
3 eggs, beaten
1 tsp. vanilla

Tie cinnamon and cloves in cheesecloth bag. Pour 2 cups milk into top of double boiler, add spice bag and heat over boiling water for 20 minutes. Remove spices; add rice and cook until rice is tender, about 45-60 minutes. Add remaining 2 cups of milk, salt, sugar, eggs and vanilla. Stir thoroughly and pour into buttered individual custard cups or a large buttered baking dish.

Set baking dish(es) in a pan containing 1" of water and bake in a 350 degree oven until pudding is set, about 30 minutes. Serve warm or chilled. (Currants or raisins may be added with sugar and eggs.)

6-8 servings

In Sweden, this dessert is served at Christmastime with Lingonberry Sauce (see index).

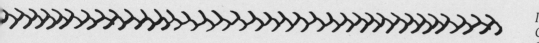

Australian
Lemon Pudding

1 c. sugar
1 T. soft butter or margarine
2 T. flour
2 T. lemon juice
grated rind from 1 lemon
2 eggs, separated

Cream the sugar and butter together. Add flour, lemon juice and grated rind. Beat egg yolks and add to mixture. Whip the egg whites until stiff and gently fold into other ingredients. Pour into one 6" buttered dish or four 3" ramekins, then place in a larger ovenproof dish containing 1" hot water. Bake at 350 degrees for 30 minutes or until nicely browned.

4 servings

This pudding was made on a wood burning stove in the olden days.

English
Plum Pudding

Prepare 4 to 6 weeks before Christmas.

1 lb. citron
½ lb. candied lemon peel
½ lb. candied orange peel
½ lb. pitted dates
1 c. blanched almonds
1 lb. currants
1 lb. seedless raisins
1 lb. seeded raisins
1 pt. brandy
2 c. sifted flour
1 tsp. cinnamon
¼ tsp. ground cloves
¼ tsp. ground ginger
¼ tsp. nutmeg
¼ tsp. mace
1 tsp. salt
1 lb. ground beef suet
1 c. fine dry bread crumbs
4 eggs
4 oz. currant jelly

Hard Sauce:
½ c. soft butter
2 c. powdered sugar
1 tsp. brandy or vanilla

Finely cut the citron, lemon and orange peel, dates and almonds. Place in a large mixing bowl and add the currants and raisins. Pour the brandy over the fruit mixture and let soak for 24 hours, stirring frequently. Sift the flour, spices and salt together and mix with the suet and bread crumbs. Combine this mixture with the fruit. Beat the eggs until very light and stir into mixture. Then stir in currant jelly.

Grease well 1 large or 2 small steamed pudding molds (coffee cans can be used, using foil as a cover). Pour batter into molds, secure covers tightly, and place in large kettle with water reaching ⅓ up on the mold. Bring water to a boil, cover and simmer gently for 4 hours. Check frequently to make sure water has not evaporated. When done, unmold and wrap in cheesecloth well moistened with brandy. Wrap in foil and refrigerate until Christmas. To serve, put pudding back in molds and steam as above for 1 hour. Serve with Hard Sauce.

To make Hard Sauce, beat butter and powdered sugar until smooth. Flavor with brandy.

12-16 servings

A lot of work, but a real Holiday treat and tradition.

German
Schaum Pudding

1 c. sugar
¼ c. cornstarch
1½ c. water
½ c. orange juice
juice and grated rind from 1
  lemon
3 egg whites

Custard Sauce:
1½ c. whole milk
½ c. sugar
3 egg yolks, lightly beaten
1 tsp. vanilla

Mix sugar and cornstarch in saucepan, add liquids and grated lemon rind. Cook and stir until it looks thick and transparent; cool. Beat egg whites until stiff and fold into the cooled pudding. Chill 2 hours.

For custard sauce, blend milk, sugar and egg yolks in the top of a double boiler over hot water. Stir constantly until custard coats spoon. It will thicken as it cooks. Add vanilla. Chill 2 hours.

To serve, spoon pudding into sherbet or sauce dishes and pour custard sauce over pudding.

8-10 servings

Pakistani
Carrot Halva

A Sweet Dessert

¼ c. raisins
few strands Spanish saffron
2 tsp. hot water
1 lb. carrots
5 c. milk
1 c. sugar
¼ c. butter
¼ c. sliced almonds
cardamom powder, freshly
  ground

Wash and dry raisins. Soak the saffron in hot water. Grate carrots as finely as possible. Bring milk to a boil and add grated carrots; simmer, stirring occasionally, and cook about 2 hours or until thick and creamy. Add the sugar and raisins and cook a while longer. Add butter and saffron and continue cooking until the halva is a rich golden color. Place in bowl and sprinkle with almond slices and cardamom powder. Serve cold.

4 servings

Southern
Pecan Pie

¼ c. soft butter
½ c. sugar
1 c. light corn syrup
dash of salt
3 eggs
1 c. pecan halves
9″ unbaked pie shell
sweetened whipped cream

Cream butter to soften; add sugar gradually and cream until fluffy. Add corn syrup, beat well. Add salt and eggs, one at a time, beating well after each addition. Add pecans. Pour into pie shell and bake in 350 degree oven for 50 minutes or until a knife inserted in center of filling comes out clean. Cool and serve with whipped cream.

8 servings

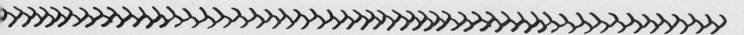

Italian
Rice Pie

Crust:
½ c. soft margarine or shortening
½ c. sugar
3 eggs
2½ c. flour
1 tsp. baking powder

Filling:
1 c. regular rice (not instant)
1 qt. milk
1 c. sugar
1 T. vanilla
1½ lb. ricotta cheese
6 eggs
chocolate chips or citron
 (optional)

For crust, cream margarine, sugar and eggs. Add flour and baking powder. Roll out dough to fit into two 9" pie pans.

For filling, boil rice in milk until tender. Add sugar and vanilla; cool. Add ricotta cheese and eggs, mix well with beater. Chocolate chips may be added, if desired. Pour filling into pastry-lined pans and bake at 350 degrees until knife comes out clean, approximately 40-50 minutes.

Yield two 9" pies

A special Easter dish.

Pennsylvania Dutch
Shoofly Pie

½ T. baking soda
¾ c. boiling water
½ c. light or dark molasses
1 egg yolk, well beaten
9" unbaked pie shell
¾ c. flour
½ tsp. cinnamon
½ c. brown sugar
1/8 tsp. each nutmeg, cloves and
 ginger
½ tsp. salt
2 T. shortening
1 c. sweetened whipped cream

Dissolve soda in boiling water. Add molasses and egg yolk. Pour into unbaked pie shell. Combine flour, cinnamon, brown sugar, spices and salt with shortening, using hands to work into crumbs. Sprinkle mixture on top of liquid in pie shell. Bake in 400 degree oven about 10 minutes or until crust starts to brown. Reduce to 350 degrees and bake about 30 minutes or until firm. When cool, cut and serve topped with whipped cream.

Yield one 9" pie

American
Green Tomato Pie

3 c. sliced green tomatoes
1⅓ c. sugar
3 T. flour
¼ tsp. salt
4 tsp. grated lemon rind
6 T. lemon juice
3 T. butter
¾ tsp. cinnamon
pastry for 9" two-crust pie

Combine first eight ingredients in bowl. Place mixture in pastry-lined pie pan. Cover with top crust and pierce with fork. Bake at 450 degrees for 10 minutes; reduce to 350 degrees and bake 30 minutes more.

6-8 servings

Great for those late Fall tomatoes that never ripened.

American
Buttermilk Pie

Scandinavian
Molasses Cream Bars

American
Brownies

1½ c. sugar
3 T. flour
2 eggs, beaten
½ c. melted butter or margarine
1 c. buttermilk
2 tsp. vanilla
1 tsp. lemon juice
9" unbaked pie shell

Mix sugar and flour and add beaten eggs. Next, pour in melted butter and buttermilk. Fold in vanilla and lemon juice. Pour mixture into pie shell and bake in a 375 degree oven for 60-70 minutes or until knife inserted in center comes out clean.

6-8 servings

Almost as good as chocolate pie.

1 c. light or dark molasses
7 T. melted butter or shortening
1 egg
6 T. hot water
2 c. flour
¼ tsp. salt
1 tsp. ginger
1 tsp. cinnamon
1 tsp. baking soda

Icing:
2 c. powdered sugar
3 T. cream
¼ tsp. lemon extract

Mix the first nine ingredients together in order given. Bake in a greased 9" x 13" pan at 350 degrees for 25 minutes. Cool and frost with icing made by mixing powdered sugar, cream and lemon extract together.

Yield 2 dozen bars

1 c. butter
4 oz. unsweetened chocolate
4 eggs
2 c. sugar
1 c. flour
2 tsp. vanilla
1 c. chopped nuts

Frosting:
2 c. powdered sugar
2 T. cocoa
2 T. soft butter
1 tsp. vanilla
3-4 T. strong hot coffee

In a large saucepan, melt together butter and chocolate. Remove from heat and cool. Stir in eggs, sugar, flour, vanilla and nuts. Mix well. Pour into greased 9" x 13" pan. Bake at 350 degrees for 25-30 minutes.

For frosting, combine powdered sugar and cocoa. Add butter and vanilla and enough hot coffee to make spreading consistency. Frost cooled brownies and cut in 1" x 2" bars.

Yield 4½ dozen

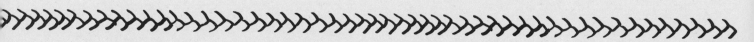

Jewish
Passover Brownies

1 c. granulated sugar
½ c. soft butter
¼ c. cocoa
2 eggs, separated and beaten
¼ c. milk
¼ tsp. salt
½ c. matzo cake meal
powdered sugar (optional)

Mix granulated sugar, butter and cocoa together. Add egg yolks, milk, salt and matzo cake meal; fold in egg whites. Pour into greased 8" square pan and bake at 350 degrees for 30 minutes. When cool, dust with powdered sugar, if desired.

Yield 1-1½ dozen bars

Good enough to make all year long.

American
Depression Fudge

2 (1 oz.) sq. semisweet chocolate
⅔ c. milk
2 c. sugar
2 T. butter
1 tsp. vanilla

Shave or cut chocolate in small pieces; add milk. Cook, stirring constantly until well blended. Add sugar. Stir mixture until it comes to a boil. Continue to boil, without stirring, to 234 degrees or until a very soft ball is formed when dropped into a cup of cold water. Remove from heat, add butter and vanilla. Without stirring, allow to stand until lukewarm. Beat until fudge loses its gloss and pour quickly into buttered 8" x 8" pan.

Yield 2 dozen pieces

American
Perfect Divinity

2½ c. granulated sugar
½ c. light corn syrup
½ c. water
2 egg whites
1 tsp. vanilla
½ c. chopped walnuts (optional)

Combine sugar, corn syrup and water in a 2-quart saucepan. Cook to 236 degrees or soft ball stage. Stir only until sugar dissolves. Meanwhile, beat egg whites until stiff peaks form. When syrup reaches 236 degrees, gradually add *half* of syrup to egg whites, beating at high speed on electric mixer. Cook remaining syrup to 250 degrees or hard ball stage and slowly add to the egg whites, beating constantly. Add vanilla and beat until candy holds its shape (this could take 5 minutes or more). Add walnuts, if desired. Drop by teaspoonfuls onto waxed paper and swirl top.

Yield 4 dozen pieces

Universal

Aunt Daisy's Love Cake

4 oz. kisses
25¢ worth sweet lips, pressed
    together
2 oz. love
½ oz. teasing
½ oz. squeezing

Combine above ingredients and bake well. Handle with care and serve warm in a happy home.

Continuous servings

You don't have to go to the store for these ingredients.

Universal

A Happy Home

2 c. love
2 c. loyalty
2 c. friendship
1½ c. forgiveness
2 T. tenderness
5 tsp. hope
4 qt. faith
1 pt. laughter
1 gal. work

Mix the love and loyalty together thoroughly with the friendship. Blend well with forgiveness, tenderness and hope. Add faith, stir in laughter alternately with the work. Bake in lots of sunshine.

Yield many generous helpings of happy years.

standard equivalents

Pinch or dash = less than 1/8 teaspoon
2 teaspoons = 1 dessert spoon
3 teaspoons = 1 tablespoon = ½ fluid ounce
4 tablespoons = ¼ cup = 2 fluid ounces
5⅓ tablespoons = ⅓ cup = 2½ fluid ounces
8 tablespoons = ½ cup = 4 fluid ounces
12 tablespoons = ¾ cup = 6 fluid ounces
16 tablespoons = 1 cup
2 cups = 1 pint
4 cups = 1 quart
2 pints = 1 quart
4 quarts = 1 gallon
11 quarts = 1 peck
4 pecks = 1 bushel
8 ounces = 1 cup
16 ounces = 1 pound
2 cups liquid = 1 pound
4 cups flour = 1 pound
4 cups unsifted powdered sugar = 1 pound
2 cups granulated sugar = 1 pound
2¼ cups brown sugar, packed = 1 pound
2 cups solid meat = 1 pound
2 cups butter or shortening = 1 pound
1 cup uncooked wild rice = 4 cups cooked
1 cup uncooked regular rice = 3 cups cooked
1 cup uncooked instant rice = 2 cups cooked
1 cup whipping cream = 2 cups whipped cream
1 medium lemon = 2-3 tablespoons juice
1 medium orange = ⅓-½ cup juice

oven temperatures

F = Fahrenheit   C = Celsius
275°F = 135°C
350°F = 175°C
400°F = 205°C
425°F = 230°C
500°F = 260°C

slow oven — 250 degrees to 350 degrees
moderate oven — 350 degrees to 400 degrees
hot oven — 400 degrees to 450 degrees
very hot oven — 450 degrees to 550 degrees

metric measures conversions

volume

ml = milliliter
1 tsp. = 5 ml
1 T. = 15 ml
2 T. = 30 ml or 1 fl. oz.
1 c. = 240 ml or 8 fl. oz.
1 pt. = 480 ml or 16 fl. oz.
1 qt. = 960 ml or 32 fl. oz.

liquid

metric pt. = 16.9 oz. or 500 ml
metric qt. = 33.8 oz. or 1,000 ml or 1 liter
metric ½ gal. = 59.2 oz. or 1,750 ml
   or 1.75 liter

weight

Gm = Gram   Kg = Kilogram
1 oz. = 28 Gm
1 lb. = 454 Gm
2.2 lb. = 1,000 Gm or 1 Kg

weights, measures & metrics

American Cancer Society Says
EAT
SMART

1. **Avoid Obesity** (may reduce risk of uterine, breast, gall bladder, colon cancers)

2. **Eat A Varied Diet** (a varied diet eaten in moderation offers the best hope in lowering your risk of cancer)

3. **Include A Variety of Vegetables And Fruits In The Daily Diet** (may reduce risk of colorectal, stomach, esophagus, larynx, lung cancers)

4. **Eat More High-Fiber Foods Such As Whole Grain Cereals, Vegetables And Fruits** (may reduce risk of colon cancer)

5. **Cut Down On Total Fat Intake** (may reduce risk of breast, prostate, colon cancers)

6. **Eat Less Smoked, Salted and Nitrite-Cured Foods** (may reduce risk of esophagus, stomach cancers)

7. **Greatly Restrict Alcohol Consumption, If You Drink At All** (may reduce risk of throat, liver, larynx, esophagus, oral cancers, and possibly other cancers, such as breast, pharynx, and stomach)

For more information call toll-free 1-800-227-2345

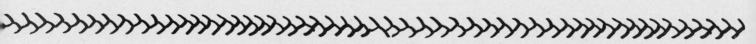

nutritional information

5 a Day – for Better Health!

Did you know that eating 5 fruits and vegetables each day is one of the most important choices you can make to help maintain your health? Since 35% of all cancer deaths can be attributed to the typical American diet which is too high in fats and too low in fiber, eating more fruits and vegetables could be the most important life-style change you ever make.

5 Points to Remember

Eat five servings of fruits and vegetables a day.

Eat at least one vitamin A rich selection (such as tomato, tangerine, winter squash, or apricots) every day

Eat at least one vitamin C rich selection (such as kiwifruit, cantaloupe, Brussels sprouts, or potatoes) every day

Eat at least one high fiber selection (such as oranges, broccoli, mango, or beans) every day

Eat cabbage family (cruciferous) vegetables several times a week

Eat Fruits and Vegetables

Nature's Fast Food!

Today's busy lifestyles often demand that fruits and vegetables be fast and easy to prepare in order to eat the recommended five servings a day. And what could be more convenient than frozen, canned, dried, or precut fruits and vegetables?

Here are some quick tips for fruit:

- Check out the supermarket salad bar for prepared melons, fresh pineapple, and other ready-to-eat fruits.

- Getting 1 of your 5 is as easy as grabbing an individual serving of 100% juice instead of soda.

- Sliced peaches, pineapple or pears are only a can opener away! Look for those packed in 100% juice.

- For a quick, handy snack, try dried dates, figs, prunes, raisins, apricots, and others.

Here are some quick tips for vegetables:

- Buy precut carrots, celery, broccoli and cauliflower at your supermarket salad bar.

- Frozen or canned vegetables need only to be put in a bowl and covered before heating in the microwave.

- Trimmed and cleaned spinach leaves, lettuce leaves, baby carrots, and shredded cabbage are available in supermarkets for salads or snacks.

- Microwave a vegetable (potato, yam, sweet potato) by rinsing, piercing it with a fork and popping it into the microwave.

- Always prepare your fruits and vegetables with minimal added fat and salt. And remember –

5 a Day for Better Health!

American Cancer Society Tips for Preparing Food

- Bake, poach, steam, oven-broil, stir-fry, or roast meats, poultry, and fish without using extra fat. Avoid frying, which adds extra fat and calories.

- Ask your butcher to help you select lean cuts of meat. Trim away all visible fat, and use 2–3 ounce portions. Cut meat into thin slices to look like more. Remove the skin from poultry.

- Use vegetable cooking sprays instead of frying in fat.

- Cook vegetables as quickly as possible and use as little liquid as you can.

- Use herbs and spices, onion, garlic, ginger, lemon and lime juice, and mustard instead of butter, fat, and oil to flavor meats and vegetables.

- Use the paste method for gravy or sauces. Add flour or cornstarch to cold liquid slowly and blend well. This eliminates the need for fat.

- After making a soup or stew containing meat or poultry, refrigerate until the fat congeals on the surface. Remove it before heating or serving.

- Substitute skim or non-fat milk for whole and yogurt for sour cream whenever possible. Choose desserts made with milk or yogurt instead of those made with cream. You might find that you prefer dishes and desserts that aren't too rich.

- Use "comparison shopping" to select recipes. Pick the recipe that contains the least amount of fat. Even then, most fat in recipes can be reduced by 1/3 to 1/2. This works well for casseroles and main dishes, as well as for quickbreads, muffins, and cakes.

- Try adding a little bran or wheat germ to recipes, even casseroles and main dishes. Every little bit helps.

- Experiment and have fun. Add additional fruits and vegetables to recipes for extra fiber and vitamins. Try new — and healthier — combinations of foods.

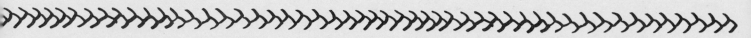

American Cancer Society Tips for Grocery Shopping

- Change your eating and shopping habits gradually. Think of it as an ongoing process of good health for life. It's just not possible to learn everything about healthier lifestyles at once, so don't set an impossible task for yourself.

- Try to plan shopping as carefully as possible. Sometimes, shopping has to be done in a hurry, but try to give some thought to it ahead of time in order to minimize or eliminate impulse purchases. Besides, even a few moments of planning saves a lot of time and aggravation at the store. Spend some time in advance thinking about healthy substitutions and additions to make.

- Avoid shopping on an empty stomach.

- You don't have to avoid treats or rewards. Just try to think of healthy foods as special treats.

- Explore the produce section. Be adventuresome and try a new kind of fruit or vegetable. Try them one at a time, so they won't seem as overwhelming. Think of new ways to try produce, and remember that it is usually low in fat and high in fiber.

- Look for fresh herbs to season foods instead of fats, sauces, and gravies.

- A variety of foods is important to healthy eating and will also keep shopping from seeming so routine.

- Read labels carefully. Ingredients are listed in order of quantity. Choose products that have no fat or oils, or in which fats are listed last.

- Beware of so-called "healthy" or "lite" foods. Read the labels carefully for fat, fiber, and vitamin content. Remember that you don't need to buy any special foods to improve your diet.

- Avoid processed, salt-cured, smoked, and nitrite-cured meats and foods. Always buy fresh when you can.

- Select low-fat, non-fat, and skim milk dairy products.

- Buy tuna packed in water, not oil.

- Brace yourself for a barrage of impulse items, such as candy bars, at the checkout. Prepare in advance to resist this assault by reading a magazine, balancing your checkbook, or engaging in conversation.

Cut Down On Fat

One way to "CUT DOWN ON" fat is to review your favorite family recipes and to make substitutions that will be healthier — without affecting their taste appeal. Small recipe changes here and there can do much for your well-being.

INGREDIENTS	FAT GRAMS	SUBSTITUTIONS	FAT GRAMS	
1 oz. Hard Cheese	9 gm/oz.	1 oz. Lowfat Processed Cheese	2	gms/oz.
		2 Tbsp. Grated Parmesan	3	gms/oz.
		1 oz. Lowfat Cheese (Mozzarella, Farmers, Pot, Part-Skim Ricotta, or Cottage)	5	gms/oz.
1 Whole Egg	6 gms/oz.	¼ cup Egg Substitute	0	gms/oz.
		2 Egg Whites	0	gms/oz.
1 cup Whole Milk	9 gms/cup	1 cup 2% Milk	5	gms/cup
		1 cup 1% Milk	3	gms/cup
		1 cup Skim	0	gms/cup
1 cup Sour Cream	40 gms/cup	1 cup Lowfat Yogurt	2	gms/cup
		1 cup Lowfat Cottage Cheese, puréed	4	gms/cup
1 cup Regular Mayonnaise	179 gms/cup	1 cup Reduced-Fat Mayonnaise	64	gms/cup
		½ cup Lowfat Plain Yogurt & ½ cup Reduced-Fat Mayonnaise	33	gms/cup
1 cup Whole Milk Ricotta Cheese	32 gms/cup	1 cup Part-Skim Ricotta	20	gms/cup
		1 cup Regular Cottage Cheese	10	gms/cup
		1 cup Lowfat Cottage Cheese		
1 cup Heavy or Whipping Cream	90 gms/cup	1 cup half-half	27	gms/cup
		1 cup Evaporated Whole Milk	19	gms/cup
		1 cup Evaporated Skim Milk	1	gms/cup
1 cup Ice Cream	14 gms/cup	1 cup Ice Milk	6	gms/cup
		1 cup Sherbet	4	gms/cup
		1 cup Frozen Yogurt	4	gms/cup
1 oz. Cream Cheese	10 gms/oz.	1 oz. Neufchâtel Cheese	7	gms/oz.
		2 Tbsp. Puréed Lowfat Cottage Cheese	.5	gms/oz.

when ye can't seek or find

if you're out of:	you can use:
spices/flavorings	
½ tsp. cayenne or red pepper	few drops Tabasco
1 T. chopped fresh herbs	1 tsp. dried herbs
1 tsp. dry mustard	2-3 tsp. prepared mustard
1 T. lemon juice	2 tsp. vinegar
1 tsp. grated fresh ginger	¼ tsp. ground ginger
1 clove garlic, pressed or minced	¼ tsp. instant minced garlic or 1/8 tsp. garlic powder
½ c. chopped fresh onion	2 T. instant minced onion
1 tsp. Italian seasoning	¼ tsp. each oregano, basil, thyme and rosemary plus dash of cayenne
1 tsp. pumpkin pie spice	½ tsp. cinnamon, ¼ tsp. ginger, 1/8 tsp. each nutmeg and cloves
1 tsp. marjoram	1 tsp. oregano
1 tsp. Worcestershire sauce	1 tsp. bottled steak sauce
fresh parsley	fresh celery leaves
flour/starches	
2¾ c. cake flour	2½ c. all-purpose or unbleached flour
1 T. cornstarch or 1½ tsp. arrowroot	2 T. flour
leavening agent	
1 tsp. baking powder	1 tsp. cream of tartar plus scant tsp. baking soda

substitutions

if you're out of:	you can use:
vegetables	
1 lb. fresh mushrooms	3 oz. dried mushrooms or 6-8 oz. canned mushrooms, drained
1 c. canned tomato sauce	8 oz. can stewed tomatoes blended in blender or 1 c. tomato puree, seasoned
1 c. tomato juice	½ c. tomato sauce plus ½ c. water
broccoli flowerets	cauliflower or Brussels sprouts
cooked pumpkin	cooked squash
fruits	
1 c. raisins	1 c. cut-up dates, currants, dried prunes or snipped apricots
1 c. sliced fresh strawberries	10 oz. pkg. frozen strawberries, reducing sugar in recipe to ⅓ c.
meats	
½ lb. ground pork	½ lb. sausage meat
1½ c. diced cooked ham	12 oz. pork luncheon meat, diced
½ lb. shrimp, cooked, shelled and deveined	5 oz. canned shrimp
nuts	
pine nuts	sunflower seeds
cashews	peanuts
miscellaneous	
½ c. ketchup or chili sauce	½ c. tomato sauce plus 2 T. sugar, 1 T. vinegar and 1/8 tsp. cloves
½ c. tartar sauce	6 T. mayonnaise or salad dressing and 2 T. pickle relish
white wine	apple cider or juice
1 c. chicken or beef broth	1 c. water plus 1 bouillon cube or 1 tsp. instant bouillon

if you're out of:

sweeteners

1 c. honey

1½ c. corn syrup

1 c. sugar

1 c. brown sugar

¼ c. cinnamon-sugar

chocolate

1 (1 oz.) square unsweetened chocolate

1 square semisweet chocolate

4 oz. bar German's sweet chocolate

dairy products

1 c. whole milk (fresh)

1 c. buttermilk or soured milk

1 c. dairy sour cream

shortening

1 c. butter or margarine

you can use:

1¼ c. sugar plus ½ c. water

1 c. sugar plus ½ c. water

⅔ c. honey plus ½ tsp. baking soda

½ c. granulated sugar plus ½ c. molasses plus ¼ tsp. baking soda

¼ c. granulated sugar plus ½ tsp. cinnamon

3 T. cocoa plus 1 T. fat

1 square unsweetened chocolate plus 1 T. sugar

¾ c. real chocolate chips

½ c. evaporated milk plus ½ c. water or 1 c. reconstituted nonfat dry milk plus 2 T. butter or oil

1 T. vinegar or lemon juice plus whole milk to make 1 cup (let stand 5 minutes)

1 c. plain yogurt or 1 c. evaporated milk plus 1 T. vinegar or 1 c. cottage cheese mixed in blender with 2 T. milk and 1 T. lemon juice

7/8 c. oil or lard or ¾ c. rendered chicken fat

where it's at

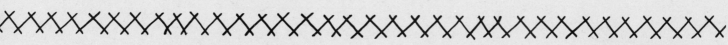

index

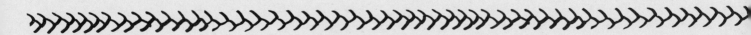

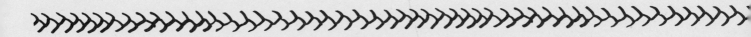

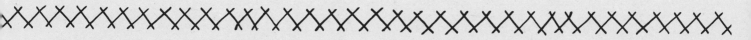

thanks to all who shared and cared . . .

Kristine Aasheim, Eve Aberman, Ellan Adams, Gloria Bonato Aho, Lillie Aga, Heljo Alari, Mrs. S.E. Alm, Carol Anderson, Donna Anderson, M/M George Anderson, Mrs. Wendell Anderson, Abby Andreason, Barbara Aranjo, Margaret Arnar, Mrs. Arthur Arndt, Lorrayne Aysta, Tena Ayer / B Dalton Bookseller, Ida Bach, Toni Bacon, Ferol Baertsch, Judy Baker, Gladys Bakken, Judy Baron, Mrs. Donald Bauer, Muriel Bauman, Ginger Baumchen, Judith Bell, Elisabeth Bennett, Aimee Berg, Betty Berg, Mrs. Chester Berg, June Berg, Delma Bergland, Shirley Besikof, Lorraine Bestiel, Eleanora Bischoff, Mickey Bix, Matta Bjornson, Helen Bjorsness, Arline Bloom, Pat Board, Roberta Bockovich, Ann Bodger, Mrs. Edwin Boeder, Ethel Boetlcher, Darlys Bohnsack, Andrea Bolger, Jack Bolger, Norman Booth, Jr., Mrs. Rudy Boschwitz, Darline Bourn, Helen Bradford, Mrs. Gaylord Bridge, Norma Brodeen, Mrs. E.W. Broden, Marnie Brodt, Helga Brogger, Mary Jo Browne, Lois Bruckschen, Pat Bryant, Nancy Bubalo, Grandma Buettner / Tom Campbell, Sr., Margaret Cantwell, Dorie Carey, M/M A.M. Carlson, Corine Carlson, Hilda Carlson, Margaret Carlson, Sharon Carlson, Nellie Carman, Denice Carpenter, Barb Carriger, Flo Casey, Margie Casey, Sasha Cervenka, Sharon Chauss, Delores Chazin, Teresa Chen, Jane Christofferson, Maxine Chupurdin, Pat Chupurdin, Lucille Clark, Lucille Clem, Alma Coleman, Sherley Confeld, Marion Conlin, Mrs. Artie Cook, Sharon Cook, May Corniea, Rosa Coronado, Mary Corrada, Jeanne Corwin, Grandma Crist / Ruth Danielson, John Dargan, Mrs. David Davis, Lois Davis, Mrs. Harold Davison, Lenore Dawson, Ileana De Ghendt, Alex Dekker, Olivier Pierre Deleval, Mrs. Louis Delmonico, Mary DeLong, Mrs. Philip Deraas, Ginny Dessal, Florence Deutsch, Mitzi Diamond, Franklin Dickson, III, Ann Dietrich, Maribeth Dittberner, John Dizon, Jane Dorn, K. Dougall, Mrs. Jim Douglas, Maria Drowly, Duffey Paper Co., Ernestine Dullum, Penny Durenberger, Sue Dusenka / Gordon Eckre, Mrs. Edward Edel, Edith Edelman, Elvera Edin, M/M/ Shlomo Elancry, Louise Erickson, Mary Erickson, Marge Evenson, Mrs. George Ewens / Lee Fabian, Helen Farmer, Mrs. John Faust, Mrs. Herman Feldman, Mrs. Norman Feldman, Helen Felt, Delores Fenney, Marie Fesenmaier, Ruth Field, R.A. Fischer, Susie Fiterman, Jan Fogt, Dorothy Foster, Yvonne Foster, Jean Fournier, Mrs. Bennett Fox, Attee Franzen, Grace Fredrickson, Margie Freeman, Ruth Frenzel, Ida Friedell, Mrs. Eddie Fristad, Ann Fuller, LaVon Funck / Leona Gacke, Fran Gakemeier, Millie Gallager, Mrs. John Gallos, M/M Narcissus Garcia, Mrs. Clinton Garlock, Miriam Garvis, Sarah Garvis, Lou Gerber, Mary Gertsner, Theone Gilbertson, Kathy Ginad, Mrs. H. B. Gislason, Barit Gjerde, Konnie Goege, Bonnie Goetzke, Rivoli Golden, Mrs. C.J. Goldsmith, Laverne Goldtel, Barri Gordon, Baylee Gordon, Gerry Gossen, Evelyn Goulette, Mrs. E. Gozdonovich, Enid Grindland, Mary Gross, Wanda Gunderson, Barbara Gudmundson, Marian Gustafson, Mary Jane Gustafson / Mrs. Henry Hagen, Mrs. Edwin Hakel, Mrs. John Halbersma, Sally Hall, Gail Halverson, Erva Hance, Paul Hanes, Barbara Hansen, Jennie Hansen, Laura Hanson, Eunice Harriman, Mary Harris, Edna Hart, M/M Rusty Hastad, Lillian Havenstein, Pauline Haydak, Mrs. Walter Hecht, Martha Hedine, Constance Hedtke, Hekla Club, Leila Helmke, Mary Hemmersbaugh, Mayme Henderson, Joyce Hendrick, Mary Hennen, Maxene Hennum, Mrs. E.R. Herman, Valerie Herschman, Mrs. Arnold Higdem, David and Marcia Hinitz, Sandy Hoag, Mrs. Ralph Hodnik, Janne Holen, Marge Holl, Mrs. Roger Holtrop, Ann Holm, Sandy Holm, Gael Holzer, Mary Hoppestad, Mary Horbul, Mrs. George Horish, Dorothy Horns, Kay Horsch, Mrs. Owen Hughes, Bess Hum, Mrs. Hubert H. Humphrey, Marjorie Hundeby, Mrs. Leonard Hurst, Signe Hurst, Eldoris Hustad / Helen Ingvalson / M. Jacobson, Lorraine Jamar, Lucille Jasinski, Ivy Jensen, Kay Jensen, Victor Jensen, Mrs. Frank Jerabek, Etta Johnson, Carmen Johnson, Carol Johnson, Mrs. Craig Johnson, Doreen Johnson, Mrs. Lawrence Johnson, Lorraine Johnson, Mrs. R.O. Johnson, Mrs. Roy Johnson, Sue Johnson, Vicki Johnson, Joy Johnsrud, Alice Jones, Tom Josephson, Amy Judkins, Mickey Judkins, Eleanor Julkowski / Corin Kagan, Edla Kalander, Hans Kalitzki, Alice Kansanback, Alyce Kawauchi, Marlene Kayser, Margaret Kelen, Marcia Kells, Helen Kelley, Joyce Kent, Minnie Keyser, Mary Beth Kibort, JoAnn Kinzer, Adeline Klein, Dianne Kline, Carol Knops, Charlotte Knoss, Joan Knight, Estelle Knudsen, Mrs. Dennis Knutson, Laura Koebnick, Hilda Kontala, Johanna Kooyenga, Heldi Korts, Jerre Koschak, Ada Koski, Delores Kottie, Dorothy Krob, Mrs. Sidney Kruger, Dorothy Kuch, Mary Kuehethau, Betty Kuhl, Gloria Kurkowski, Mrs. Frank Kuttner, Judy Kuusisto / Mrs. Al LaBelle, Elaine Labelle, Mrs. W. Lah, Carole Landa, Eleanor Lapidus, Mrs. Bruce Large, Ada Larsen, Ann Larsen, Carol Larson, Claudia Larson, Florence Larson, Marlene Larson, Ray Larson, RoxAnn Larson, Mrs. Warner Latick, Mary Lynn Leff, Rick Leser, Mrs. Halyna Lewytskyj, Joan Libodean, Miriam Liberman, Floyd and Margaret Lien, Bernice Lindahl, Ann Lindquist, Pat Lindquist, Lillian Lindstrom, Louis Locketz, Susan Lofquist, Gladys Logelin, Bowyer Lowrenz, Aino Lukk, Barbara Lundgren, Jan Luoma, Cecilia Lynch / Catherine MacKondy, Sharon McCarty, Charlene McCoy, Kathy McEnaney, Mrs. W. G. MacFarlane, Peggy McGee, Lucy McHale, Nancy Mckay, Libby McKeon / Mrs. Con Maanun, Jr., Janice Machau, Mrs. Peter Magrath, Margaret Majewski, Betty Manke, Minnie Manke, Mrs. Sherman Mankell, Dorothy Manske, Sarah Mankoff, Clara Marihart, Mrs. Kenneth Martens, Eleanor Martin, Mrs. Roger Matti, Cari Mayo, Hiram Mendow, Jo Mendow, JoAnn Menk, Diane Mersch, Iria Mestits, Minnie Metzger, Verna Meyer, Patty Middleton-Miller, Julie Midtaune, Barbara Mikelson, Kari Mikkelson, Mrs. Marty Milbrandt, Ann Miller, Mrs. Charles Miller, Mrs. Lloyd Miller, Mrs. Rudolph Miller, Debbie Minde, C. Miska, Klaus Mitterhauser, Helen Moehn, Joan Mondale, Sara Monick, Nan Moonen, Gen Moore, Lee Moral, Ginny Morgan,

contributors, testers, helpers

Margaret Morris, Mrs. Milton Moxness, Ruth Moyer, Mary Mueller, Rosemary Mueller / Ella Nachbar, Florence Nanoff, Harriet Neitge, Annette Neff, Cibby Neff, Verna Neilsen, Ellen Nelson, Kathleen Nelson, Phoebe Nelson, Corky Neuman, Joanne Newhart, Betty Newman, Louise Newmann, Eileen Newton, Lois Neys, Nhung Ngo, Bryn Maria Nichols, Vivian Nick, Mrs. Verlyn Nickle, June Nordgren, Alice Norland, Karen Norsby, Lyllis Northey, Mrs. A.W. Nuetzman, Shirley Nygaard, Mrs. Peter Nygaard / Mrs. John Ohlemann, Mrs. Louis Ohlen, Marilyn Olin, June Olsen, Karen P. Olson, Kay Olson, Margie Olson, Phyllis Olson, Shirley Olson, Jody Onell, Mrs. Redgie O'Nel, Mary Orr, Jim Oxberry / Jean Paciott, Packaging Corp. of America, Sheila Paisner, Lois Palmer, Shirley Palmer, Mrs. A. Papas, Janet Parker, Mollie Patinkin, Marlys Paulson, Betty Penner, S. Penner, Mrs. Harold Pepperling, John Pergakis, Mrs. Rudy Perpich, Rae Pesek, Jerry Peterson, Gertie Peterson, Philoptochus Society of St. Mary's Greek Orthodox Church, Vylla Picotte, Adelyn Pierson, Dorothy Pink, Jane Pistner, Mrs. Clarence Podratz, Mae Pokorney, Lorna Potter, Mrs. S. Prelesnik, Mrs. George Pribyl, Carolyn Pulju, Mrs. D. Puncochar / Donna Qualey, Gretchen Quie, Joyce Quinn / M. and D. Radulovich, Angelina Rahn, Caryl Range, Ella Rask, Carolyn Reil, Mrs. Gelman Resset, Tita Ricks, Larry Riley, Hal Rindal, Terry Rivard, Mary Roberts, Gert Robertson, Ellen Rockbar, Sarah Rockler, Mrs. Edwin Roeder, Mary Ann Rogers, Esther Rogner, Kathy Rosebrock, F. Everett Rosemond, Mrs. Robert Rosenberg, J.J. Rosenzsweig, Tudie Ross, Marilyn Rovner, Margaret Rudeen, Carolyn Rulus, Delores Runge, Nora Rust, Lorraine Rustari, Georgiana Ruzich, Mrs. D.F. Ruzicka, Marlys Ryti / Mrs. N.M. Salute, Mrs. James Schmidt, Mrs. Louis Schmiesing, Jenny Schuler, Jan Schultz, Lillian Schulz, Shelley Segal, Mrs. N.J. Sehr, Helbe Perandi Seller, R. Gail Seifer, Meda Sexton, Carole Ann Shadle, Shirajoy Shandleing, Doris Sherman, Mrs. Evan Shogren, Mrs. Richard Skanse, Krystyna Skrowaczewski, Dr. Melvin Sigel, Margot Siegel, Selma Sievert, Earle Smith, Jeannie Smith, Wilma Soehern, Gladys Soehren, Linda Sorensen, Marie Spee, Janet Spoor, Vi Stafford, Carol Stagness, Roz Steinfeldt, LaRayne Steinke, Rocelia Stene, Peggy Stephens, Mrs. T. Stole, Mrs. Orville Stordahl, Mrs. A. Stroening, Babs Strom, Dan Stroman, Phyllis Sudit, Harold Sumner, Ernest Swanson, Carol Swartz, Mrs. Clifford Swenson, Bonnie Syverson, Joni Szarzinski / Tartan Imports, The Bookmen, Inc., Mary Thieman, Mrs. Emlyn Thomas, Mrs. Axel Thompson, Myrtle Thompson, Mrs. Lowell Thorson, Dorothy Thovson, Joan Tibodeau, Donna Tiede, Marjorie Tjepkem, Joanne Topp, Jim Toscano, Mary Toscano, Sharon Toscano, Bonnie Totino, Rose Totino, Linda Towle, Van Tran, Naah-Troutner, Margaret Tucker, Mary Tuttle / Mrs. W.M. Ullevig, Marge Ulstad, Roger Ulstad, F. Urseth / Frances Vacek, Mrs. Ray Valek, Ruth VanDelinder, Mrs. P. VanderMolen, Isa Van Helden, Rosa Vargas, Peggy Vermes, Mrs. George Vigen, Marjorie Vogt, Carol Voorhees / Mrs. Art Waha, Rita Waletski, Mercy Walker, Fern Wagen, Ann Warhol, Lil Warschauer, Jill Waterhouse, Elaine Weber, Eileen Wegerson, Lori Weidich, Velma Weil, Lillian Weinandt, Joanne Weiner, Lillian J. West, Ginny White, Gayle Whitesell, Angie Wiemerslage, Mrs. W.C. Williams, Glen Wilmot, Mrs. Dick Wilson, Peg Wilson, Doloris Wing, Rev. and Mrs. M. Witte, Philomena Wodash, Mrs. Elden Woken, Judy Wolf, Mrs. Jack Wolfson, Dinah Wolson, Joan Wong, Mrs. Loren Woodke, Elizabeth Woodward, Mrs. T.R. Wuerzberger / W.M. Yllevig, Eleanor Yokiel / Maiji Zaeska, Dora Zaidenweber, Betty Zats, Dr. Alvin Zelickson, Ann Zelle, Mrs. E.E. Zemke, Pat Ziebarth, Bernice Zipperman, Grandma Zwilling / Jeni Born, Carol Ruth Geissal, Judy Kuller, Harry Linduff, Dr. James Myhre, Ann Phillips, Linda Ruckman / Twin Cities Home Economists in Business and its members from the following companies: General Mills, Inc., Green Giant Co., International Multifoods, Land O'Lakes, Inc., Litton Microwave Cooking, National Supermarkets, Sylvia Ogren — Consultant, / Minneapolis Area Vocational Technical Institute / Moon Kim, Jean Johnston, Sharon Howell, Carol Ruth Geissal, Carol Owens, Joan McDonald, Vida Neidorf, Andrea Chesney, Lillian Goldfine, Jan Edmunds, Donna Funk, Mary Helen Delong, Ernestine Dullum, Joy Linduff, Florence Nanoff, Gladys Logelin, Lorraine Johnson, Lisa Knutson, Louise Jones, Marge Shaw, Lorraine Diamond, Jan Edmunds.

Even though not every recipe made the printed page, we wish to thank all the contributors, testers, tasters and helpers who answered our plea and made this cookbook a reality.

If we have inadvertently omitted your name, please add it on this provided space: _____

For the sake of posterity, add your own family favorites . . .

January 1993

The McIlhenny Company proudly declares that

Minnesota Heritage Cookbook
hand-me-down recipes

a cookbook from
The American Cancer Society
Minnesota Division, Inc.
has been selected to the
Walter S. McIlhenny Hall of Fame

This award is given to recognize a uniquely American book form —
the community cookbook — and the committed volunteers who use
it so effectively to benefit charitable causes. This cookbook provides
a record of regional culinary culture and improves the quality of
community life with the funds it generates. This community
cookbook has documented sales of over 100,000 copies since it was
first published.

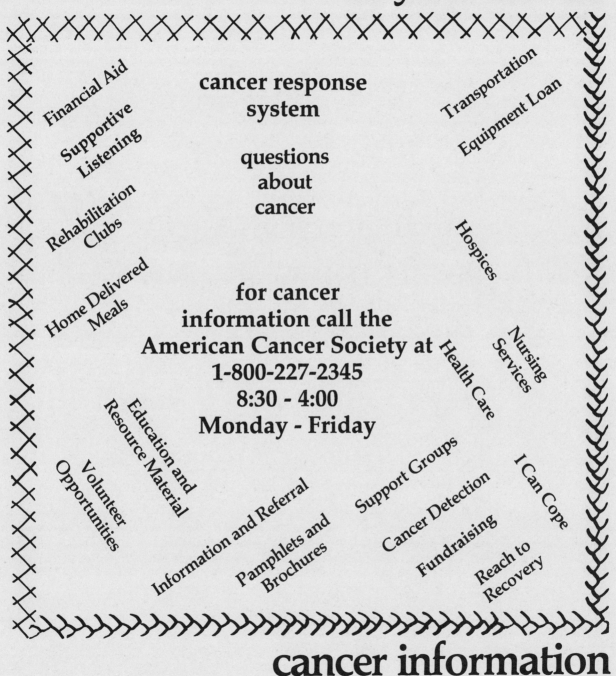

at your service

cancer response
system

questions
about
cancer

for cancer
information call the
American Cancer Society at
1-800-227-2345
8:30 - 4:00
Monday - Friday

Financial Aid

Supportive
Listening

Rehabilitation
Clubs

Home Delivered
Meals

Education and
Resource Material

Volunteer
Opportunities

Information and Referral

Pamphlets and
Brochures

Transportation

Equipment Loan

Hospices

Nursing
Services

Health Care

Support Groups

Cancer Detection

Fundraising

I Can Cope

Reach to
Recovery

cancer information

help keep us cookin'

Minnesota Heritage Cookbook
VOLUME I
hand-me-down recipes

edible nostalgia
a culinary legacy
a family heirloom

Order forms are provided for your convenience. For each cookbook, please send $15.95 plus postage and handling charges of $3.00 for 1 book and $2.00 for each additional book.

Call 1-800-582-5152 (MN only) or 612-925-2772 to charge on Visa, MasterCard, or American Express, or make checks payable to the American Cancer Society and mail to 3316 W. 66th St., Minneapolis, Minnesota 55435.

On gift orders please enclose your own gift card and instructions on where to send books. **Thank you very much!!!!**

order forms

AMERICAN CANCER SOCIETY
Minnesota Division, Inc.

Help keep us cooking . . .

Please send [   ] Minnesota Heritage Cookbook, Volume I

[   ] Minnesota Heritage Cookbook, Volume II

Contribution per book @ $15.95 _____

Postage and Handling: $3.00 for first book and $2.00 for each additional book _____

Total enclosed _____

Send to:

Name _____ Phone (day) (____)_____ (eve) (____)_____

Address _____

City, State, Zip Code _____

Make checks payable to *American Cancer Society* and mail to: 3316 West 66th Street, Minneapolis, MN 55435

Phone orders: 1-800-582-5152 (Minnesota only) or 612-925-2772

Please charge to my ❑ VISA ❑ MASTERCARD ❑ AMERICAN EXPRESS

Card Number _____ Expiration Date _____

Cardholder's Signature _____

On gift orders, please enclose your own gift card and instructions on where to send books. **Thanks much!**

AMERICAN CANCER SOCIETY
Minnesota Division, Inc.

Help keep us cooking . . .

Please send [   ] Minnesota Heritage Cookbook, Volume I

[   ] Minnesota Heritage Cookbook, Volume II

Contribution per book @ $15.95 _____

Postage and Handling: $3.00 for first book and $2.00 for each additional book _____

Total enclosed _____

Send to:

Name _____ Phone (day) (____)_____ (eve) (____)_____

Address _____

City, State, Zip Code _____

Make checks payable to *American Cancer Society* and mail to: 3316 West 66th Street, Minneapolis, MN 55435

Phone orders: 1-800-582-5152 (Minnesota only) or 612-925-2772

Please charge to my ❑ VISA ❑ MASTERCARD ❑ AMERICAN EXPRESS

Card Number _____ Expiration Date _____

Cardholder's Signature _____

On gift orders, please enclose your own gift card and instructions on where to send books. **Thanks much!**